Macbeth!

Mini Book Series

VOLUME XXXI

By

Ronald Pattinson

Copyright © 2017 Ronald Pattinson

1st edition

Published in August 2017 by

Kilderkin
171 hs Warmondstraat, Amsterdam, Noord- Holland

ISBN 978-94-90270-32-2

Contents

Mini Book Series

What started out as a way of collecting together my blog posts into a series of small books. Mostly for my own convenience, but with the thought in the back of my mind that I might be able to shift a few.

As I wrote more and more blog posts – which I added to the initially quite small volumes – I soon ended up with books which weren't very mini at all. And as I thought of more themes to assemble my posts under, the number of books began to grow, too. The initial set of eleven had soon doubled in number. I'm now up to volume XXXI. Even I struggle to remember all the titles.

Doubtless – unless I'm hit by a tram next week – there will be more volumes to come. There's just so much I want to write about. And my list of beery obsessions grows ever longer. Feel free to buy them all. Then I might be able to retire early. Which has been my dream since, er, I started working.

Amsterdam, July 29th 2017.

UK

Macbeth comes to Macclesfield

Past weekend was a momentous day in the history of the universe. I kicked off my latest book pimping exercise.

I enjoyed traipsing around the USA so much trying to get an incomprehensibly reluctant public to buy my effing book, I thought I'd give it another go. This time with my vaguely coherent (as opposed to nailed together blog posts) new self-published job about Scottish beer.

I use the word coherent in its loosest sense. Though neatly divide into chapters, the number-side of the book is so overloaded, it lists scarily to port. Or starboard. Not totally sure which the number side of a book is.

Scotland. I've banged on about for so long banging out a book on it seemed bang on. Save me loads of arguments, I hope. And maybe even earn me thruppence hapenny back. A more than fair reward than for the thousands of hours with my nose pushed up the pasts' arse.

It all started a couple of months ago.

"Do you fancy going to Macclesfield, Dolores?"

"Where's that?"

"Just outside Manchester, it looks really nice."

"That's not why you want to go there, is it, Ronald?"

"It's only twenty minutes from Manchester by train."

"You're planning one of your boring talks, aren't you?"

"Fascinating insights into beer history is how I prefer to bill them."

"Hah – you admit it."

"You got me there, Dolores. It'll be fun. There's hills and everything in Macclesfield."

"I grew up with hills. Do they have nice beer? Not that horrible grapefruit juice. Nice Bitter."

"Of course. It's the North. They may even have Mild."

That swung it.

Macclesfield here we come.

Macbeth comes to Macclesfield (part two)

I'm learning how to plan my travel. To make it as painless as possible. Which is important when you travel as much as I do.

We're staying opposite Piccadilly Station. Dead handy for a couple of reasons. It's in the centre of the city. The train from the airport goes there. And the trains to Macclesfield leave from it. I make that several wins.

The event in Macclesfield doesn't start until 13:00. Leaving plenty of time for a few cups of tea and a Greggs bacon sandwich before jumping on the train. We drop down in the nearest carriage, but soon move on. It's a bit smelly. And not totally clean. Not good, as it's going all the way to the South coast. We move on to a different carriage that's slightly less stinky. God knows what state it will be in by the time it reaches its final destination.

The journey gives Dolores a chance to see how big a built-up area Manchester is. It's solid until past Stockport. Then we pop out into a countryside of steep, dark green hills, the distance misted through rain. It looks lovely. If a bit soggy. I've a very soft spot for the northern landscape. Especially when it starts getting a bit wild.

We've deliberately arrived a little early to give us a chance to look around the town a little. I'm dead impressed by the view that greets us as we leave the station: a square blackened church atop a hill. Below it a broad landscape of pubs. My sort of town.

"We could go for a drink, Dolores. Except none of the pubs are open." I'd already noted that all had their doors closed. "Since they let pubs open all afternoon, they've started opening later. I bet they all open in five minutes." It's 11:55.

Sure enough the red doors of the Nags Head open up at noon. Our choice of pub is made.

There are a surprising number of people inside, including several small children. It soon becomes obvious that these are various generations of the landlord's family. It's a Robinsons pub.

"It's ages since I've drunk any of their beer. What do you want, Dolores?"

"Just get me a nice Bitter."

No surprises there. Dolores loves her cask Bitter. We have different Bitters, but both are pretty good. Served through a sparkler, the mouthfeel is soft and tender, like a loving kiss.

A group of men drinking Carling assembles on the table next to hours. They're in their forties and fifties. It soon becomes obvious that they're a group of Man United fans warming up for the afternoon's game.

We only stay for the one. To give us time to give the town the once over. Just one problem: it's up a dirty great hill.

Hills have played a minor role in my life. Newark, where I grew up, has one token hill. But it's on the edge of town. No need to climb it. Mablethorpe, where I spent most summer weekends in my youth, is even flatter. Literally as flat as Holland, being Dutch-built polder. The last thirty years of living in Holland has left me totally out of tune with hills. It's a struggle climbing up it.

"At least it'll be downhill on the way back." I say.

It's worth the climb, just about. A typical smallish English town, without too many jarring modern intrusions into the townscape. The grand neoclassical town hall is a demonstration of past civic pride.

We potter around the shops for a little. Until it's just about showtime.

Next: the debut gig of my year-long international Macbeth tour.

Macbeth comes to Macclesfield (part three)

At 12:45 we head over to Five Clouds, the beer shop where I'll be speaking. There are a few people milling around inside, which is a good sign. If half a dozen can be said to be milling.

I make myself known and am immediately offered a beer. Which is a very good sign. The event itself is taking place downstairs in the cellar. It's, er, cosy. I can understand why attendance has been limited to just over a dozen.

On one table stand all the beers we'll be trying. I'm dead impressed with the effort they've gone to. Some lovely adaptations of genuine William Younger labels. Appropriate as many of the beers were originally brewed by William Younger.

Rather than send out random recipes, I've sent the people taking part in the Macbeth project sets of themed recipes. For Macclesfield, that was Shilling Ales. The recipes are a mix of 1847 and 1868 William Younger and 1894 Thomas Usher. They've brewed the 1847 Younger beers, plus 80/- and 100/- from both breweries.

There's no projector, which means everyone will have to look at the slides on my laptop screen. Not ideal but, as I said, it is quite cosy down here.

While we're waiting for a few latecomers to toodle up, I chat with the club members. At 13:15 we decide to kick off, despite not everyone being there. It's actually not that clear a break between the chat and the talk. Not that that bothers me.

This is my first go with this particular talk. It's got rather more slides – 60 - than my usual 45-minute jobs. I wonder how long it will take. I'm aiming for around an hour. Which turns out to be hopelessly optimistic.

At several points we break to try the beers. Gives my voice a rest and slakes my thirst. And doubtless relieves the boredom of hearing me drone on and on.

The beers are pretty good, though a couple are a bit on the fizzy side. All are dangerously drinkable, despite their strength. Even Dolores likes them and she's quite choosy. And not usually that keen on the strong stuff.

After just three hours, I'm done. I've noticed Dolores fidgeting and tapping her watch for about the last two hours. Do you think she's been trying to tell me something?

Once we're all packed up, Mike Gaskell, who organised everything, and a couple of club members take me and Dolores for a few beers and a bite to eat in the town. Go on. If you twist my arm I'll drink some beer.

Rather than trad pubs, we head for a couple of newer-style drinking establishments. First, it's the Treacle Tap, a narrow long bar that has a bit of the look of a café. But obviously a much better beer selection. It's got handpulls, which pleases Dolores. She has her usual pint of Bitter.

We both eat pies, which are really dead good. Best pie I've had in a while. The kids would love that. Though somehow I doubt they will ever be in Macclesfield. But you never know.

Next stop is RedWillow, which also has its own brewery. It's a much roomier place than Treacle Tap. Evidently it used to be a furniture shop. They've quite an array of their own beer, which is nice. Especially as they have handpulls as well as keg taps. Dolores would strangle me if I took her somewhere with only evil keg.

We're at the bottom of the hill, thankfully. It's a leisurely and flat walk back to the station.

Everyone else on the train seems to be going for a night out in Manchester. Two young lads are necking some spirit and cola combination from a pop bottle. While a group of young lasses in sparkly miniskirts pass around a bottle of wine. I wonder what state they'll be in on the way home?

As a special treat, here's one of the beers that was brewed for the event:

1868 William Younger 100/-		
pale malt	17.75 lb	100.00%
Cluster 90 min	2.00 oz	
Saaz 60 min	2.00 oz	
Saaz 20 min	2.00 oz	
OG	1076	
FG	1034	
ABV	5.56	
Apparent attenuation	55.26%	
IBU	69	
SRM	6	
Mash at	154° F	
Sparge at	185° F	
Boil time	105 minutes	
pitching temp	57° F	
Yeast	WLP028 Edinburgh Ale	

Five Clouds
8 Market Pl,
Macclesfield SK10 1EX.
http://www.fivecloudbrew.co/

The Treacle Tap
43 Sunderland Street
Macclesfield
SK11 6JL
01625 615938
http://www.thetreacletap.co.uk/

Opening Hours:
Mon-Thurs : 16:00 - 23:00
Fri - Sat : 12:00 - 00:00
Sun: 12:00 - 23:00

RedWillow Bar
32a Park Green,
Macclesfield,
Cheshire, SK11 7NA
http://www.redwillowbar.com/

Opening Hours:
Monday Closed
Tue - Thur 16:00 - 23:00
Fri - Sat 12:00 - 24:00
Sun 12:00 - 22:30

Macbeth comes to Manchester

Gig number two of the trip is in Manchester itself. At Beer Nouveau which, conveniently, is within walking distance of our hotel.

But we kick off on the other side of town. At the John Rylands Library. I've been past the building plenty of times. It's a pretty hard to miss ornate pink stone gothic pile. Unless you're so fixated on your phone you never lift your eyes from the pavement. Dolores wanted to take a look at an exhibition there and have a look around the library itself.

Wanting to keep up the pretence of this trip not being just about beer, I said "Yes, brilliant."

It wasn't a lie. Not about the exhibition, but the building itself. I fancied a closer look at that.

(Did I mention my thing about buildings? It's what I dream about, mostly. That missing buses/trams/trains/planes or losing all my computers.)

Like many old public buildings, some idiot decided to move the entrance from its logical and architectural signalled position at the front to a bland modern shed tacked onto a rear corner. Presumably so they could add a gift shop you can't avoid. I really hate this sort of shit. Demonstrates both a lack of understanding and lack of respect for the older structure.

The modern extension is unlike the original building in very way. Every wrong and bad way. Trying really, really hard, you couldn't come up with something less sympathetic. Bland and sterile is about the nicest way I can describe it. Though the phrase "turd atop a pie" is lurking around in the back of my mind.

The original building is gorgeous, if you like the wedding-cake intricacy of high neo-Gothic. I've come to appreciate it myself, after a somewhat sceptical start. The contents are equally impressive. Especially the weird old medical tomes they have on display.

The reading niches are beautiful and full of natural light. Great places to study. If it weren't for the drip, drip water torture of passing gawpers. Of which I'm one, sadly. How the hell could you concentrate while being photographed by random passersby? Including me, sadly.

An hour or so in there's a strange rasping in my throat. Must be all those dusty old books drying it out.

"Time to go to the pub, Dolores? My liver thinks I've turned teetotal."

"There's no chance of that, Ronald." Dolores says. Accompanied by one of those looks.

Being lunchtime, Dolores agrees. We'd decided earlier that we'd be lunching at The Moon Under Water. We thought we'd splash out on a fancy Wetherspoon's meal.

I quite like The Moon Under Water. Mostly because, being pretty huge, you're just about guaranteed to find a table. It's surprisingly quiet for 13:00 on a Sunday. Just the odd pensioner reading a paper. I blame all-day Sunday opening. When I were a lad I'd be jangling my change and shuffling from foot to foot at 11:45 every Sunday. You had to take advantage of every single minute of the 120 the pubs were open.

It's a bit of a bummer that Wetherspoons have dropped Sunday dinners. But a steak and kidney pud will do just fine. I'm a man of simple tastes. Dolores goes for a meal with a pint option.

As I've told you tediously often, Dolores is a big fan of cask Bitter. Nothing fancy, just standard cask Bitter. It has to be cask, mind. None of that keg or smoothflow rubbish. She's actually more doctrinaire on this point than me. I get her a pint of Ruddles Best and myself something a bit more crafty. Mostly because it's the strongest cask beer they have.

When I get back to our table, I notice that my pint isn't settling out. It looks like chocolate milk shake, except more cloudy. And thicker. I'm pretty sure that it isn't meant to look like that. But you can't be certain nowadays with all these trendy unfined beers.

(On a side note, just because a beer hasn't been fined is no excuse for it pouring as murky as a pint of mud. A well-brewed beer should drop bright with or without finings, if left to settle long enough.)

I take it back to the beer and tell the friendly teenage barmaid that I think there's something wrong with my beer.

"Isn't it supposed to look like that?", she asks in mellifluent Mancunian tones.

"I don't think so." I say, trying to sound confident. I'm old, so she'll probably believe me.

"Is this right?" she asks an older colleague, who confirms that the barrel needs changing. Phew. I didn't fancy arguing the toss on that one. What is the world coming to when you can't be sure that a pint of sludge isn't quite right?

I get a new pint of another beer.

There's something very soothing about a Wetherspoons during a quiet patch. That tempts you to stay for several slow pints, while outside the world whizzes on at its usual frantic pace. Or maybe it's just the cheap beer. I'm a bit of a sucker for that. And why I usually avoid crazily-priced evil keg.

Back in our hotel, I've time to polish off a couple of the leftover beers from yesterday's event.

"I have to drink them, Dolores. We can't take them back." Which is true, as we've flown Easyjet and have no check in bags.

"Right, Ronald." She says, giving me a very cynical look.

Beer Nouveau next. And an encounter on Temperance Street.

The John Rylands Library
150 Deansgate,
Manchester M3 3EH, UK
Tel: +44 161 306 0555
http://www.library.manchester.ac.uk/rylands/

The Moon Under Water
68-74 Deansgate,
Manchester M3 2FN, UK
Tel: +44 161 834 5882
https://www.jdwetherspoon.com/pubs/all-pubs/england/manchester/the-moon-under-water-manchester

Macbeth comes to Manchester (part two)

Beer Nouveau as an easy stroll from our hotel. All we need to do is follow the railway line running from Manchester Piccadilly.

It takes us along the ironically named Temperance Street. Which is Beer Nouveau's official address. As we're walking down the, to be perfectly honest, rather desolate street, I hear someone call "Ron" behind me.

It's Matt Thompson, a fellow blogger who will be attending the event*. He gets me to pose below a Temperance Street sign. I can't imagine why.

When we arrive at the brewery, there are already a few people there, sampling the historic beers that have been brewed for the occasion. It's more Shilling Ales, though not the same ones as in Macclesfield.

Steve Dunkley, the man in charge at Beer Nouveau, quickly puts a beer in my hand. Steve has been doing some interesting things with wooden casks. Putting beer in them, mostly, which I guess doesn't sound that interesting. But it is when you have exactly the same beer served from a plastic cask using a beer engine and by gravity from a wooden cask. I wouldn't have believed what a difference it could make, had I not experienced it myself.

I'm pleased to say that a few brewers have taken an interest in oak casks. Definitely something to watch out for. Who said SPBW was irrelevant?

I've time for a few beers while I wait for the final stragglers to show up. Which I'm not going to complain about. That was, after all, one of the points of setting this whole trip up: getting to drink beers from historic recipes. How else would I get the chance?

Happily there's a projector for me this time. Makes life much easier. I positively rattle through the talk, finishing in just 2 hours 45 minutes. That's a full 15 minutes quicker than yesterday. Clearly it's going to need some editing before I take it to the US later in the month.

We have a few more drinks when I'm done talking before trailing back to our hotel. I finish off a few more of bottles that I've acquired. Can't take them on the plane is my excuse.

* You can read Matt's account of the event here:

http://whenmyfeetgothroughthedoor.blogspot.nl/2017/04/macbeth-in-manchester.html

Beer Nouveau
Temperance Street Brewery
75 North Western Street,
Manchester, M12 6DY.
http://beernouveau.co.uk

USA

Amsterdam to Holland

Things haven't started well.

I get to Schiphol two hours before my flight to Chicago is due to start boarding. Plenty of time for a leisurely couple of beers before jumping on the plane. I suspect things may not be that simple when I need to queue to join the baggage drop-off queue. It's a foretaste of things to come.

I get a false sense of reassurance when I'm able to get my bag checked in in under 20 minutes. Then I spot the queue for the security queue. This is crazy. The security queue extends right down the stairs. I'm in for a long wait.

After the first half hour, there's something hypnotic about how the queue slowly snakes back and forth along the tape barriers. I don't think I'd be having such a zen experience if time was tighter until my flight.

Finally I get to the head of the queue . . . and am redirected to another queue by the security point itself. Then I notice I'm in the longest of said queues and people who were in the main queue are getting through before me.

As happens every time at Schiphol, one of my bags is plucked out for extra attention. This time it's my electric toothbrush causing concern.

By the time all the faffing about is done, I've just about time to buy my traditional bottle of Laphroaig in the duty free and arrive at the gate as my flight begins to board. My worst ever experience at Schiphol by a long way.

Safely aboard, the crew announce the flight will be delayed for 30 minutes while they remove the luggage of twelve passenger who haven't shown up. Presumably stuck in the security queue.

I start to fret a little. There are only four hours between my scheduled arrival time in Chicago and the departure of my train. You never know how immigration will take. In Newark once with Dolores and the kids it took over two hours.

Chastened by my experience is Asheville, when I nearly got stranded, I have a plan B. Should I miss my train, I know could get a Greyhound to Holland tomorrow. It would be tight, but I could still make it on time for my first event of the trip.

I pass the time, as usual, by watching crap films on the entertainment system. It's amazing how quickly the time can pass when you head is immersed in brainlessness.

We land at O'Hare pretty much on schedule. I deplane as quickly as possible and rush to immigration. Am I in the right spot? Where is everyone? Amazingly, there's no queue. No grilling from the officer at the desk and I'm through, passport freshly stamped, in under five minutes. If only it were always that speedy.

Getting through so quickly means I need to wait for my checked-in bag. Now there's a novelty when arriving in the US.

Soon I'm in a taxi rolling down the long, desolate, and often overcrowded, concrete highway that leads from airport to city. As with many US airports, it's a long way out of town. It's not the quickest of journeys, but I've still plenty of time before my train. Just as well I've made contingency plans for this eventuality, too.

As part of Plan A, I've identified the nearest reasonable-looking pub close to the station. Close being the most important criterion. Giving the slightly unweildly luggage I'm lugging. It's Dylans Tavern & Grill, a pseudo-Irish pub just a block away. Busy with an after-work crowd, the hostess finds me a small table.

The beer selection isn't the greatest, but there's one standard I can rely on: Sierra Nevada Pale Ale. I order that and a burger. I can relax, at last. Let the buzz wrap around me as I wrap my chops around the burger. Life can be good at times.

Amish crowd the station's waiting room. Or are they Mennonites? Not sure I can tell the difference. All to do with the colour of their hats, evidently. So does that mean trains are OK, while cars aren't? It must be an odd world to inhabit. But maybe no odder than mine.

Amtrak carriage may be getting long in the tooth, but they do offer plenty of room. A plug by every seat. And decent strength free wifi. Could be much worse.

We trail through suburban Chicago for quite a while, through the usual industrial flotsam that floats around railway tracks the world over. Once free of the city's embrace, massive, rusting chunks of industry still line our path and we skirt Lake Michigan, crossing the state line in the process. I watch the orange glow of the sun as it sinks over the lake, placid in dusk's calm. Like a distant reflection of the rusting factories.

I'm surprised when Holland is announced an hour earlier than I expect. "Is that right?" I ask the conductor. "I thought we weren't scheduled to arrive until 10:30?" He explains that we also changed time zones when we crossed into Michigan.

Kevin Hilgert, of New Holland brewery, is there to meet me at the station. It's not far to my hotel, but I still appreciate a lift with all my luggage.

Once I'm safely checked in, we head over to the New Holland brewpub. It's not far. Then again, New Holland isn't a very big town. We have a few beers. Until I begin to fade and it's time for bed.

Tomorrow is my first gig. It's going to be a busy few days.

Dylans Tavern & Grill
118 S Clinton St,
Chicago,
IL 60661.
http://dylanstavernandgrill.com/

New Holland Pub on 8th
66 East 8th Street
Holland,
Michigan 49423.
http://newhollandbrew.com

Holland, Michigan

It's worked. I stayed up long enough yesterday to sleep right through until morning US time.

That's my usual plan. Get acclimatised as quickly as possible. Not that I'm in any rush this morning. I've arranged to meet my man in Holland, Kevin Hilgert, at 13:30. Being incredibly lazy, I choose Big E's Sports Grill. It's on the ground floor of my hotel. In my defence, it does offer 80 draught beers.

Kevin's a little late, but that's no biggie. There are plenty of TVs for to have a staring contest with as I slowly assimilate a beer. There's even a Premier League game showing.

That's one of the biggest changes since I lived in the USA 30 years ago: the hugely increased visibility of football in general, but English football in particular. Though, being honest, I'm happy enough the watch baseball. Not much chance of seeing that it Amsterdam. At least not professional US games. And Dolores is recording Match of the Day for me.

Kevin arrives and gets himself a beer. "Would you like to try some other spots in town before the event?" he asks. To be honest, I'm happy enough staying here. My schedule for the next couple of days is pretty demanding. No point making it any harder than it needs to be.

We don't have a huge amount of time, as my event bullies off at 16:00. We have a couple of beers and some food then take the long walk to the New Holland brewpub. It's all of one block. I told you Holland wasn't a big town.

Appropriately enough, some tulips decorate the street. In a few weeks there will be far more when the Tulip Time festival takes place.

http://www.tuliptime.com/daily-events/

I'm talking on the patio, as Americans like to call their beer car parks. Or fag-smoking spots, as they often are in reality.

Worrying about the equipment is part of the thrill of these trips. Will there be a screen and a projector? Will the projector have a VGA connection? And most importantly, will my laptop boot up? Though, as a last resort, I always have a copy of my slides on a memory stick. Plan for the worst is my rule. As it's quite likely to happen.

There's a decent enough crowd. Thirty at least. Unless everyone is just out here for a crafty smoke. I've tweaked the presentation since its first outing in Macclesfield and Manchester. Fewer slides and a faster pace. Shouldn't last more than two hours. Or so.

I rattle through it in an hour or so, which is what I hoped for. If not actually believed I could achieve.

Once I've batted away the questions, it's time for some beer. I do try to have a glass in my hand while speaking. But that's mostly to stop myself absent-mindedly scratching my bollocks. I'm too busy talking (when no-one can easily interrupt me) to do much in the way of drinking.

Me, Kevin and a couple of others brave the long trek to Our Brewing, another brewpub. Not a block, just a couple of doors away. A long thin single-shop unit stripped back to its brick bones.

I'm getting tired. I've a complicated, if not that long, journey tomorrow. Involving a doughnut house.

"Going down to the doughnut house, gonna get me a chocolate éclair" sings in my head as I head off to snoozeland in my coptormobile.

Big E's Sports Grill
121 E 8th St,
Holland,
MI 49423
Tel: +1 616-582-8585
http://bigessportsgrill.com/holland

Our Brewing Company
76 E 8th St,
Holland,
MI 49423.
Tel: +1 616-994-8417
http://ourbrewingcompany.com

Hillsdale, Michigan

I rise early. I need to, because of today's transport arrangements.

And I want to breakfast properly. The full egg, bacon and breakfast potato nine yards. Washed down with energising coffee. It dances a merry jig on the spot. I'm set up for the day.

My ride to Hillsdale, next stop on the tour, is a bit complicated. It's going to be a relay, with me being handed over, like a baton or a handcuffed criminal, at a doughnut house in Kalamazoo.

First leg is being carried out by Zachary and his friend. They pile me into a big truck and soon we're on our way to that most wonderfully-named of American towns: Kalamazoo. Amazingly, everything runs perfectly. As soon as we enter the doughnut shop Kevin Slack, who's taking care of the next leg, introduces himself.

A breathe a sigh of relief as we rejoin the motorway and head towards Hillsdale. You may be wondering why I'm heading to Hillsdale. It's very simple: I was asked.

I organise my US tours in a pretty anarchic way. I mention on the internet where I plan going and wait for prospective hosts to get in touch. My original plan for this trip was to fly into Chicago, spend one night there before taking the train to Milwaukee. Michigan wasn't in my plans at all. Then Kevin Hilgert of New Holland and Chris Hamilton of Hillsdale College contacted me.

Kevin is an enthusiastic home brewer, giving us plenty to chat about on our way to Hillsdale. Where we're meeting Chris at noon. In a pub, happily. The slightly oddly-named Here's To You Pub & Grub.

A couple of the pub's staff are busy outside.

"You can go inside if you want, but I can't serve you beer until noon." One of them tells us. It's 11:50. We sit down inside and content ourselves with a water for the next ten minutes. We're just starting our first beer when Chris Hamilton arrives.

Chris, a biochemist and Associate Professor of Chemistry at the college, is the very image of a clean-cut American. Also a very friendly and knowledgeable man. As a chemist he understands brewing, er, chemistry far better than I ever will. "If I went to university again, I'd study biochemistry", I tell him. "Then I might be able to understand modern brewing text books."

We have a light lunch, but don't linger long. My talk kicks off at 15:00, but the event starts 90 minutes earlier for homebrew sampling. The theme for this event is Thomas Usher beers of 1894. These beers have been brewed:

1894 Thomas Usher PA
1894 Thomas Usher IPA
1894 Thomas Usher 60/ PA
1894 Thomas Usher 60/ XX (Mild)
1894 Thomas Usher Export Stout

Yes. I'm getting to taste old Thomas Usher recipes. What better use of a Sunday afternoon?

A local and a college journalist interview me before the show. I have to talk about myself and beer history. What is there not to like?

"Is it OK if we record the talk? No problem. They rig up a tablet in a weird frame. It's pointing at me, I suppose.

It's a proper lecture hall. I get a podium and a microphone. Luxury. Obviously, the basics like projector and screen are there. Mostly taking nothing for granted works best.

A few people leave early. Not enough for it to be disheartening. I've been told it's quite a conservative college so I leave out the swearing. Only used occasionally and for emphasis, I might add. I don't eff and blind the whole time.

Chris has an appointment for an hour or two and leaves me in the hands of two of his students. They show me around the campus. I've heard it's a conservative college. Not a Conservative one. Seeing a statue of Margaret Thatcher is a bit of a shock. I manage to hold back the vomit. And the invective. "She's a divisive character in the UK." I mumble, evasively.

The museum is fun, especially as they have a real life, well real very dead, dinosaur. Who doesn't like a dinosaur?

They take me to the refectory for a meal. I must have made poor choices. The food is a bit grim.

Did I mention that I'm staying with Chris tonight. After guaranteeing me a zero cat presence in his house, I was happy to accept his hospitality.

We go back to his for a few post-event beers. A few friends, including fellow home brewers, come along, too. One is a prison officer. He gives me a coaster with the prison service logo.

"That was made by a prisoner. From an old licence plate."

Cool, I think. Alexei will love that.

We share a few beers and slowly chat the evening down. I can't stay up too late. Another complicated travel day.

Next time, I finally meet Kristen England.

Sweetwater's Donut Mill
2138 S Sprinkle Rd,
Kalamazoo, MI
http://sweetwatersdonuts.com/

Here's To You Pub & Grub
45 North St,
Hillsdale,
MI 49242.
Tel: +1 517-437-4002
https://m.facebook.com/pubandgrub/

Hillsdale to Minneapolis (via Detroit)

I rise reasonably early. Lots to do today.

Did I ever mention that I love having breakfast in old-fashioned American diners? They remind me of London cafes. The good ones. In both countries. So when Chris asks where I'd like to eat, the choice is easily made.

We sit at the counter and chat while waiting for our food. I really like Chris. Despite how odd his biscuit and gravy breakfast looks. "I expect gravy to be brown." I mention. "It's sausage gravy." He replies. No, still not getting that one. He offers me some and it tastes pleasant enough. I'm taking my usual greasy route to breakfast satisfaction.

Chris drops me at the building where I spoke yesterday. He has to give a lecture. My shuttle to Detroit airport is due in 45 minutes. I go inside and read one of the newspapers they've kindly provided. I skip the really depressing bits and stick to the "quite" and "just a bit" depressing. Nothing in the least cheery, obviously.

The "shuttle" is me and a driver. He's a former navy man and retired trucker. With quite a few stories. Just as well, given the 90 minutes we'll be sharing this vehicle. He's a good antidote to the general dismalness of the newspaper. His stories mostly have a positive ending.

Detroit airport isn't huge. Which is fine by me. The smaller the better. And with as few effing people as possible in it. Especially the latter, after my Schiphol nightmare. I have been here before, when I as in Detroit for work. But that was so long ago, I can't recall a single thing about the airport.

There's no queue at all for security. I'm through in a couple of minutes.

Which leaves me plenty of time for a drink or two at the bar. I follow my usual plan: head for the bar closest to my gate.

I order a beer and a double bourbon.

"I can't give you a beer and a double. I can pour you single then give you another one when you've drunk that." The barmaid informs me. You what? They have some crazy alcohol rules here in the US.

I'm flying with Delta. Mostly because they partner with KLM, my principal frequent flyer account. It's an uneventful flight. Which is how I like it.

While I'm waiting for my bags I hear someone say "Hey, Ron!" behind me. It's Kristen.

This is an odd moment. We've corresponded for nigh on a decade, but never met until now. The words tumble from both out mouths. Just like resuming a half-finished conversation. There's no interruption in our chatter all the way to my hotel.

I leave Kristen in the lobby while I rush upstairs to dump my stuff. When I open the bag I checked in there's a pungent smell. Beer. Half my clothes are soaked, but thankfully none has reached the books. That would have been really annoying. It's easy enough to wash clothes.

I soon find the culprits: a bottle of Butcher's Tears Spiral Scratch and one of their Isaac's Rose. The crown corks are still in place, but the bottles are 90% empty. I don't understand. They made it over the Atlantic OK. Never had a bottle leak on me before.

This is going to leave me short of clothes. I quickly rinse out the affected shirts socks and undercrackers in the bathroom. Not out of any real hopes of being able to wear then when dry. Just to stop my luggage smelling like a pub just after throwing out time.

Luckily my package of books arrived safely. The books I hope to sell tonight and tomorrow. They're in Kristen's car.

Before going to Bent Brewstillery for the event, Kristen takes me for a beer and a bite at a pub nearby. I can do with some fodder. I've eaten nothing since breakfast.

At Bent Brewstillery I first busy myself with getting the equipment ready. This time it's a big TV rather than a projector and screen.

It's starting to fill up. They don't usually open on a Monday. Meaning they must be here to see me. I hope they're in a book-buying sort of mood. The taproom is soon pleasingly full.

As I'm feeling a bit knacked, Kristen gives me a big mug of cold-pressed coffee. It seems to do the trick. Soon I'm rocking through my talk at pace. I have to keep things rolling along or it'll take hours. Best keep it to 60 minutes, at most.

Once all the questions are answered, I set about the real business of the evening: flogging my books. Not just the new Scotland one. I've brought along a few copies of the Home Brewer's Guide to Vintage Beer as well. Both sell pretty well. I'll be filling my bathtub with 100 dollar bills later. (I wish.)

I also get stuck into the beers Kristen has brewed for the event:

Stout - 1949 Younger DBS stout
IPA - Ushers 1885 IP
Keeping/Scotch - 1913 Younger No. 1
Export - 1865 William Younger Ext
Table - 1868 William Younger Teeble beer

They're very nice. The Table Beer is a surprise. Very pale and very drinkable, with the Saaz hops lending it a Pilsner quality.

We don't stay up too late. Another early start tomorrow. And a very full programme.

Next time: I regret not bothering to take my coat.

Coffee Cup Diner
73 N Broad St,
Hillsdale,
MI 49242.
Tel: +1 517-439-0140

Bent Brewstillery
1744 Terrace Dr,
Roseville,
MN 55113.
Tel: +1 844-879-2368
http://www.bentbrewstillery.com/

New Ulm

After the bottle-leaking disaster, I'm forced to review my clothing policy. Yesterday's shirt doesn't look too filthy. It'll do for today as well.

There's a long drive ahead of us, so Kristen picks me up early. No time for breakfast. Not even a cup of coffee.

We've plenty to talk about during the drive. Not all of it beer-related.

Kristen's son is already thinking about which of his three choices of national team he'll play for. His father seems more interested in which would make the most amusing headlines. Like "England humiliates England" should he play for Hungary. Though you could pick any random country. Really any random country. FFS Iceland beat England. And were the better team.

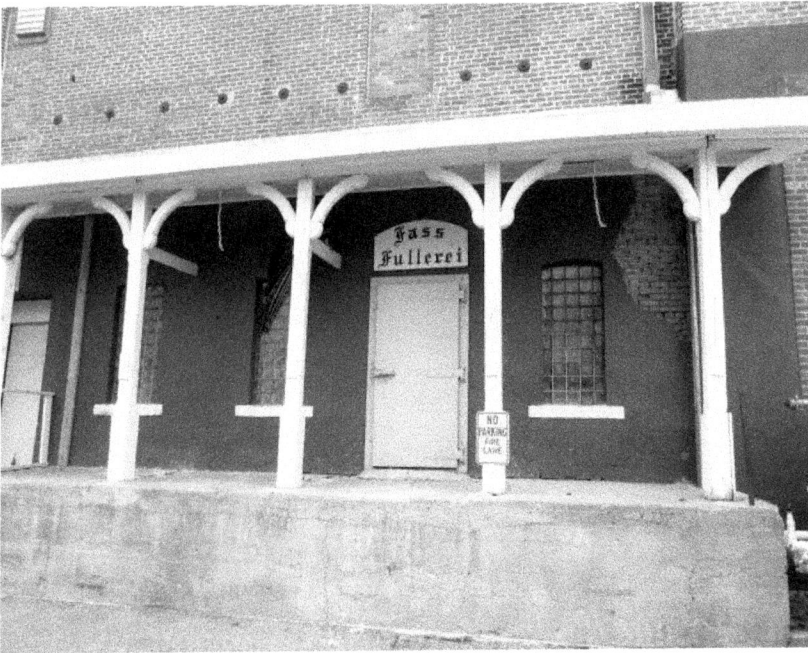

The peacocks are a bit of a shock. Not just their screechy cries. Also that they were up in the rafters of a roof. Who knew the things could fly? Their feathers look to be purely for amusement purposes only.

We're meeting Jace Marti, one of the brewers at Schells. But he isn't answering his phone. While we wait Kristen and me take a spin through the small museum. When we get to the display of coopering tools, Kristen says: "They used some of these when fixing ups the vats in the Starkeller." How cool is that?

I notice a lot of people named Marti in the family photos. George Marti married a granddaughter of the founder August Schell and became manager after both her mother and brother died in quick succession in 1911. Members of the Marti family have been involved in the brewery ever since.

When Jace turns up we have a quick chat before heading over to Turner Hall for a spot of lunch. Which I could definitely do with. Not having eaten since yesterday.

On the way over, Kristen explains what Turner Hall is. The founders of New Ulm were a group of German immigrants keen on promoting physical and mental health. Which explains the classroom and gymnasium in the hall. At first I wondered why they had the English name Turner. Then I twigged: they Anglicised a German term. The official name of the group running Turner Hall is the New Ulm Turnverein.

Being Germans, the founders remembered to put a Ratskeller in the basement. It's decorated with murals of idyllic German scenes. Evidently they've only recently been restored, having been painted over at the end of WW II.

While we eat, Jace explains about Carlsberg and Tuborg yeast. Basically all modern bottom-fermenting yeasts are derived from either the one or the other. What a nerdy conversation.

Once lunched, we pick up coffee and head for the location of my talk: Starkeller. It's not such a cellar as a barn. And is where Jace runs his sour beer programme. Stars of the cellar are 10 massive cedar vats, which used to be in the main brewery before being removed decades ago. After years of disuse they were recently repaired and put back into commission.

While we prepare for the event, Jace lets me try several of his Berliner Weisse variations.

Luckily the projector box does contain a VGA cable. Yippee! I'm all connected.

It's an MBAA meeting, with me as featured speaker. Usually, I'm pretty calm before speaking. Bit nervous, this time. As it is an audience of professional brewers, mostly, I'll be talking to. And it's a few years since I gave this talk on German sour beer styles. I hope I can remember all the muscle and fat that fills out the skeleton of the slides.

There is one heckler. Kristen, obviously. He pulls me up when I mention that the acidity in Adambier probably came from Brettanomyces.

"No, that doesn't produce so much acidity. Probably Pediococcus."

Bastard. I'm sure he's right. I'll remember for next time. If there is one.

Talk talked, I vainly try to flog some books. Despite attendance of around 100, I only sell one. Disappointing doesn't do it justice.

We return to the main brewery for dinner. It's right over the other side of town. I can understand why Jace's father didn't want it too close, what with all the bugs knocking around.

The food consists of a steak the size of a tablecloth, a potato bake thing and broccoli salad. As much meat as I usually eat in a fortnight. And a half. Or so. A lot of meat. Very nice, but an awful lot of it. I regret having that burger for lunch. Should have had something smaller. And not bothered with the chips. Oh well, lesson learned.

After eating we tour the brewery. Which is compact and packed full of interesting old stuff. Unfortunately, it's raining quite heavily. And we start outside. I wrongly assumed this morning that I wouldn't need my coat. I'm getting rather wetter and colder than I care for. It's mostly warmer inside the brewery. But not everywhere. It varies up and down dramatically, depending on the function of the particular room. Probably going to catch my death.

After the tour, we have another beer and everyone starts to melt off into the night. As Kristen and I do.

It pisses it down all the way back to Minneapolis. Just as well we're in a car. Seeing as I have no coat.

I'm looking forward to tomorrow. It's a free day. No events, no meetings no nothing. Going to be wonderful. And I'll remember my coat.

New Ulm Turner Hall
102 S State St,
New Ulm,
MN 56073.
newulmturnerhall.org
Tel.: +1 507-354-4916
http://www.newulmturnerhall.org/

August Schell Brewing Company
1860 Schell's Rd,
New Ulm,
MN 56073.
Tel.: +1 507-354-5528
http://www.schellsbrewery.com/

The Starkeller
2215 N Garden St,

New Ulm,
MN 56073.
Tel.: +1 507-354-5528

MBAA
Master Brewers Association of the Americas
http://www.mbaa.com

Minneapolis again

This is all so confusing. I can do what the hell I want today. Just need to find a late breakfast location.

Checking on Google Maps, I find a possibility within easy walking distance: Freehouse. Breakfast to beer* is their slogan. Where else could I be heading for my breakfast? Not that it's all that early. This is my free day. I could get up when the fuck I wanted. And that wasn't so early.

I really can do with a relaxing day. I've spoken four days in a row. It's hard for me to believe this, but I'm starting to get fed up with heating myself talk.

Freehouse is an easy walk from my hotel. In an area where old warehouses have been invaded by restaurants and bars. And hotels, like where I'm staying. The very stylish Hewing Hotel*. Really nice.

Minneapolis doesn't seem too effed up. Which isn't something you can say of all US cities. I can't recall seeing any derelict buildings yet.

As always, I move my lardy arse as close to the bar as I can, while squeezing my lardy gut against the counter.

"Can I get the beer menu as well, please?" I ask, after ordering my usual plate of fried artery-cloggers.

"Sure."

We'll they did coin the slogan "breakfast to beer". What did they expect me to do? Drink water?

All around smartly-dressed people are breakfasting . . . while going tippy, tappy, tip on their laptops. Honestly. Doesn't even breakfast get time for itself anymore?

IPA, 6.3% ABV
What about my beer? Well, it's IPA-ey. Lots of that tropical shit going on. It's fine for breakfast.

Bock, 6.8% ABV
It's a lovely clear mahogany colour. Smells malty and roasty. Quite smooth, but I'm not sure the roast fits with the style. It's a reasonable enough beer, mind.

I write my beer notes with the weird square pencil that was in my room. I must remember to buy a pen – I've manged to lose the one I brought – next time I have chance.

I notice there's a liquor store a block from my hotel and drop by to pick up a few beers for my planned afternoon of doing bugger all while watching baseball on TV. I only really want three or four beers. But they aren't selling singles. My best option is a mixed sixer, despite it being more beer than I need.

Kristen collects me at 16:30. But pretty soon has to drop me again, after we drop by his house for a little. He's taking his son to football practice. And drops me in a pub (The Happy Gnome) for a while. I've no problem with that. As long as I'm in a pub, I'm fine. Doesn't matter how crap the beer is, or how deafening the music, I'm fine in any pub that isn't totally populated by psychos. Half psychos is fine, but I draw the line at 75%.

I pour myself into a bar stool. One of the few empty ones. I'm there for a while. But after a while I get chatting with the nice couple (about my age) sitting next to me at the bar.

I start off with Steel Toe Dissent, a 7% ABV black beer. It's rather nice. But I try something different next, a Batch 300 from Fulton. Also 7% ABV, but this time an IPA. Both beers are from Minnesota breweries.

Not wanting to get too plastered before I've even had dinner, I switch to something lower alcohol. A Steel Toe Size 4, which is a session IPA of just 4.4% ABV. What am I becoming? Someone sensible, perhaps.

Kristen still has his son in tow when he returns. All three of us make our way to Surly. I've heard of them. Good name, not tried their beer yet, as far as I can recall.

The place is massive. But also very full. Things aren't looking good. Don't think we're going to be eating here.

Things are becoming a bit hazy. Maybe I shouldn't have had those afternoon Imperial Stouts. We go somewhere else for dinner. Town Hall Brewery, I believe. Everything's getting rather vague.

Another travel day tomorrow. Hopefully not too tiring.

* Somehow I managed to remember this as "Where breakfast and beer meet". "That's called Nelson Mandela Syndrome, dad." Alexei tells me. "Remembering false stuff."

** I paid for my room, in case you're wondering. But it is a really nice hotel.

The Freehouse
701 N. Washington Ave., Ste 101
Minneapolis, MN 55401
Tel: 612 339 7011
https://www.freehousempls.com

The Happy Gnome
498 Selby Ave,
St Paul,
MN 55102.
Tel: +1 651-287-2018
http://thehappygnome.com/

Surly Brewing Company
520 Malcolm Ave SE,
Minneapolis,
MN 55414.
Tel: +1 763-999-4040
http://surlybrewing.com/

Town Hall Brewery
1430 S Washington Ave,
Minneapolis,
MN 55454.
Tel: +1 612-339-8696
http://www.townhallbrewery.com/

St. Louis

I awake feeling rough. Like the Bonzos. Even the Session IPA couldn't save me. I need some food.

I breakfast in the rather stylish hotel restaurant. They don't seem to offer my usual grease packet. I order a brisket hash instead. At least it contains two fried eggs. Though I'm not keen on the ketchup in the hash. Not usually on the list of things I eat.

I don't feel much better after eating. Which makes packing rather a chore. And finishing off the beer I'm afraid to take on the plane. Who would have imagined drinking beer could be so little fun?

Kristen is taking me to the airport. I'm pretty early for my flight. But I don't like being pressed for time at an airport. Too stressful. We chat away like crazy all the way. Not exactly been many lulls in the conversation. We say our goodbyes at the kerbside.

Yahoo! Checking in my bag just takes minutes and I sail through security. This is how air travel should always be.

I consult an airport map. It tells me to take the driverless train thingy to my gate. It isn't that far, but fuck walking.

There's not much here. I just need somewhere for a pre-flight beer. After consulting another map, I find somewhere. A Twins-themed bar. The staff are all wearing Twins baseball jerseys. It's quiet, so they're quite chatty. I order a Surly Furious. Seems only fair, seeing as how I missed out yesterday at Surly. And was pretty furious about it.

There's in-flight entertainment so I watch some crap and/or weird TV. The flight isn't long so no time for a film.

As I head for the baggage carousel someone says: "Were you going to walk right past me?" It's Stan Hieronymus, who's picking me up. And putting me up. We wait for my bag at the carousel indicated, but it doesn't show up. This is the last thing I need. We ask at the Delta desk and they direct us to a different carousel. Where my bag is duly making the rounds. That's a relief.

Stan takes me to Urban Chestnut, an industrially-sized beer hall with a brewery around the back. Being early, it's not that full. But rather echoey. We're met by some of the brewery staff who quickly get a beer into my hand. Then take us around the shiny stuff in the backroom.

What can I say? Modern breweries from Manchester to Mexico look much the same. At least, if they've started with some money behind them. The cobbled-together ones are more idiosyncratic.

One of those showing us around is Florian, a German, though you'd be hard pressed to notice, given the smoothness of his American-accented English. He used to work in hops at AB. That's a recurring theme in St. Louis: people in new breweries who formerly worked at AB.

On the way to our next destination we drop by a drive in to get me some food. A sort of light lunch of seafood. It'll keep me running for the next few hours. I hope.

I'm speaking at Earthbound Brewing. A tiny brewery not far from the AB plant. It's on a street of tile-fronted shops that look like they date from the interwar period. A little reminiscent of older Marks & Spencer stores. Many of the buildings look like their better days are behind them, though a few trendy businesses indicate this is an area on the up.

When I say tiny, I really mean tiny. The building isn't even really a full-width single shop unit. The brewery is in what looks like a broom cupboard. The bar area could maybe hold 20 people, at a stretch.

But this isn't where I'll be speaking, thankfully. They've acquired a four-storey brick building at the end of the street. Appropriately enough, it used to the stock house of the Cherokee Brewery. When the renovation is complete, it will house both the brewery and a taproom.

It's still a bit of a mess, with building materials and bits of equipment strewn around. But at least they emptied the cellar of rubble. It had been filled from floor to ceiling. I can imagine just how much work it was removing it by hand. You can read more about the building's renovation here:

https://www.stlmag.com/arts/history/earthbound-beer-s-renovation-of-the-old-cherokee-brewery-reveals-a-lot-about-19th-century-st-louis/

Home brewers roll up with coolers and kegs. One even has an aluminium pin. They ask me to tap it. After a dozen or so futile taps, I hand the hammer over to someone stronger. Who duly bashes in the tap.

A wide range of Scottish recipes have been brewed.

1898 William Younger XX
1913 William Younger 160
1989 William Younger H 60/-
1868 Younger no 2
1898 Younger XXXX
1912 Thomas Usher IP
1909 Maclay OMS 63/-
1859 William Younger No. 3
1920 Drybrough 8d PA

I notice the 160/- from William Younger. I immediately gravitate towards the higher gravity beer. I need a bit of a wakener before start my spiel. But there's some interesting stuff in there. Especially the Maclay OMS. I've been wanting to try that recipe for ages.

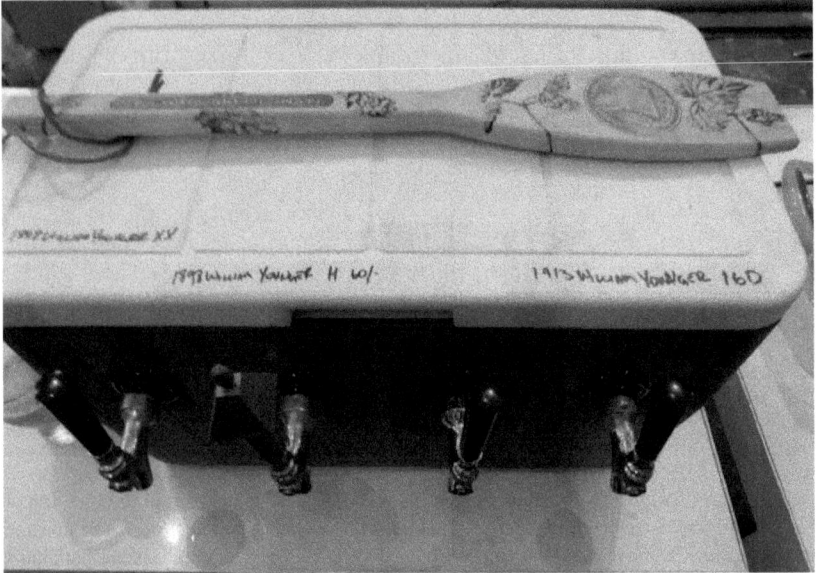

The equipment is all working and connected. I always worry about that one.

I seem to be getting the hang of this particular talk and get through to the question time in around the hour I intended. There are quite a lot of questions, from both the home and professional brewers. I don't mind. Always happy to talk beer.

Questions and chat continue after the formal formalities have been concluded. It's a knowledgeable crowd. Thankfully. No stupid questions. And I sell quite a lot of books. Just as well, given the New Ulm disaster.

After an hour or two, the crowd begins to fade away.

But we don't leave things there. I'm nothing if not game*. We head off to Nick's Pub. Bit of a beast to find a parking spot. Then we notice there's a $5 cover charge and it's mobbed with young people. Stan suggest we try elsewhere – SoHa.

It's a single-storey, strip-malley sort of building. Though it's cosy enough inside. And they sell loads of beers.

There's baseball on the TV, a buzz of conversation and I'm with friends. Happy? Think of a pig and excrement. I drink some stuff, talk some stuff and generally enjoy myself in a thank fuck all the stress is done for today sort of way.

Then Stan drives us back to his. Where I'm quickly whisked off to nodland.

Hope my laundry is done. Tomorrow could be a smelly otherwise.

* Don't know when to stop, according to Dolores.

Urban Chestnut Grove Brewery and Bierhall
4465 Manchester Ave,
St. Louis,
MO 63110, USA
Tel: +1 314-222-0143
http://urbanchestnut.com

Earthbound Brewing
2710 Cherokee St,

St. Louis,
MO 63118.
Tel: +1 314-769-9576
http://www.earthboundbeer.com/

Nick's Pub
6001 Manchester Ave,
St. Louis,
MO 63110.
Tel: +1 314-781-7806
http://www.nicksirishpub.com/

SOHA Bar and Grill
2605 Hampton Ave,
St. Louis,
MO 63139
Tel: +1 314-802-7877
http://www.sohabar.com/

Big boys and little kids in St. Louis

Another busy day ahead. But one really important task first.

Loading my dirty clothes into Stan's washing machine. I'd always planned a laundry drop here, but now it's really needed. I've a couple of pairs of rinsed and rescued socks that aren't that aren't too smelly and some undercrackers that just about pass muster. Clean shirts I'm totally out of.

Stan knows a great place for breakfast, Southwest Diner. A diner, er, that sells food from the Southwest of the USA.

Stan used to live down that way and understands the food. On his recommendation I go for a meal that combines Southwestern and St. Louis cuisine, a Southwest Slinger. A slinger is a St. Louis dish consisting of breakfast potatoes, two burger patties, melted cheese, topped with two fried eggs. The Southwestern twist are the dollops of green and red chili. Dead good. It warms me up a treat.

Civil Life is our first stop. Another single-story industrial building, though in this case surrounded by a beer garden. There are even little serving hatches so you don't have to go inside to fetch beer. Though there's no-one in the garden at the moment. It's too early. And it's raining.

The brewery concentrates on British-style beers. Which is, I guess, why Seymour, the brewer was at my talk yesterday. Soon he's pressed a glass of Wee Heavy into my heads and we head into the brewery at the rear.

It's pretty compact and boasts all the usual shiny tanks, tuns and fermenters. It doesn't take that long to tour. It isn't huge. We do our best to keep out of the way of the working brewer. A young woman who also attended my talk, who's fiddling with pipes and valves.

Before leaving, Seymour offers us some of his cask Bitter, served by handpump. It's not bad at all. Stan gets the keg version as well, so he can compare the two. He's surprised at how different they are.

We can't stay too long. Lot's still to do today. We need to make our next appointment. Which is at a slightly larger enterprise: AB.

It's still raining when we get there. Stan drops me at the beer garden while he finds somewhere to park. I roam around it looking for Rob Naylor, someone else who was at my talk yesterday. He runs the pilot brewery here. Now what did he look like? Rob appears at the same time as Stan.

Rob has his two small children in tow. It's bring your kids to work day. They're about six and eight years old, a boy and a girl. Much better behaved than my kids at that age. Mine would have kept trying to run off. Rob's follow him around obediently. Where did I go wrong?

The pilot brewery isn't such a small affair. It's a 15-barrel plant. And is designed to replicate the processes of the big kit. It has a couple of purposes. Principally to brew control batches of

Budweiser, Bud Light, etc. So they know that what they brew on the pilot replicates that of the full-size kit.

It's also used for scaling up the recipes of AB's craft purchases, such as Goose Island, to the large production facilities. That probably makes some of you a little uneasy. I can't say that it worries me.

They also produce trial and experimental batches, which sound like more fun.

After tasting, most of the beer they make is thrown away. Though some of the experimental beers are sold on draught in the beer garden.

One of Rob's experimental brews was an historic Scottish recipe of mine. I hoped I'd be able to try it today. Unfortunately they couldn't get the yeast in time and the brew is behind schedule. Bum.

Just a couple of times Rob asks me not to take photographs. Like, for example, in the hop store. I'm fine with that. It's his brewery. And I'm a nosy bastard.

I'm dead jealous of the perfect little brewery he has. Complete with an enormous lab, stuffed full of expensive equipment.

Once we're done in the pilot brewery, we take a quick spin through the main old Brewhouse. Which is absolutely gorgeous. Who takes the trouble and expense to build breweries like this anymore? Most are just sheds full of equipment.

Dodging the rain, we meet the archivist, Tracy Lauer, for a look around the museum. Lots of cool old photos and advertising stuff. Whatever you may think about AB's products, the brewery has played an important role in brewing history. Ignore the big boys and you miss a big part of beer's story.

Perennial Artisan Ales is our final brewery stop for the day. It's in a large industrial building that once produced soft drinks. The upper floors are now loft apartments, the ground floor a mix of businesses, though Perennial is gradually taking over more and more of the space. With two complete brew houses, they need a fair amount.

Brewer Jonathan Moxey is there to meet us. Impressive beard, is my first impression. They aren't open yet, but staff are scurrying around in preparation.

Would I like something to drink? Sure. I opt for Cave Torch, their flagship fruity IPA. Which also comes in actually fruited versions, I see from the menu. It's pleasant, in a fruity murk sort of way.

We look first at the original brew house, which is where all their sour beers are made. Unsurprisingly, there are many oak casks and a couple of larger vats.

The new brew house – where all the clean beers are brewed – is on the other side of the tap room. I think I'd have left a little more space between the two. Closer to 50 km than 50 m. What can I say? It's full of shiny stuff, like every brewery.

We go to a barbecue place for dinner. Pretty nice and it makes a change. Then head on to the final brewery of the day, 2nd Shift Brewing. It's a bit out of the way. Literally on the other side of the tracks. We have to dodge a huge coal train that's blocking one of the roads.

It's another shed, split in half with the taproom on one side and the brewery on the other. Not the most atmospheric of places, but my beer is fine. Stan's Pilsner, on the other hand, is a bit weird. And far too dark for the style. It turns out to have been a brewing mistake that some customers liked the taste of.

We only have the one. Though I do manage to sell a book to an acquaintance of Stan's we bump into. Yeah, another book gone.

We have another beers back at Stan's, but don't stay up late. More travelling tomorrow. I've two flights on United. Including a 45-minute change at O'Hare. Looking forward to that. Let's hope they drag me off the plane and I never have to work again.

Southwest Diner
6803 Southwest Ave,
St. Louis,
MO 63143.
http://southwestdinerstl.com/

The Civil Life Brewing Company
3714 Holt Ave,
St. Louis,
MO 63116.
http://www.thecivillife.com/

Perennial Artisan Ales
8125 Michigan Ave,
St. Louis,
MO 63111.
http://www.perennialbeer.com/

2nd Shift Brewing
1601 Sublette Ave,
St. Louis,
MO 63110.
http://www.2ndshiftbrewing.com/

Indianapolis

My flight from St. Louis is quite early. And the weather is dreadful – a heavy thunderstorm. So we leave for the airport in plenty of time. But at least all my clothes are clean.

Stan and I say our goodbyes and I do the airport formalities of check in and security. Once again it's pretty much empty and the whole process only takes a few minutes.

Time for some breakfast. I look around for options. Some of the restaurants aren't even open yet. But I can see one that is. The Budweiser Brewhouse. They do breakfast. The fatty bacony kind I love.

I plonk my bum on a barstool, as usual. I assume they have some decent beer from one of the acquisitions. But the taps I can see only offer Bud variations and Belgian stuff like Stella and Hoegaarden. Not going to drink them in the US. Sam Adams Boston Lager looks the best bet. Only when it's already been plonked in front of me do notice the taps on the other side of the bar. Featuring a distinctive long-necked goose. Bum.

The breakfast isn't the best I've had. But it's greasy enough to slip down without much problem.

I notice a Hudson as I'm walking to my gate. Ah, I remember I need a pen. Should be able to get one here. I can. But it's a St. Louis souvenir pen that costs over $5. I must remember to stop shopping in airports.

The weather is still filthy. It's announced that our flight will be delayed by 10 minutes. Not good. My change in O'Hare was already tight. It's now positively claustrophobic. I try not to fret. I'm sure everything will be fine.

It's a pretty small aircraft, two seat on one side, one on the other. But it's full. We pull away from the gate, but just hang around ion the tarmac. The crew are negotiating with the tower about their route. Can't use the original one because of the weather.

The minutes tick by. Then the pilot announces that were too heavy for the new route. We'll have to return to the gate so someone can get off. Did I mention that this is a United flight? You can imagine the sort of jokes my fellow passengers make. I pity the poor flight attendant. The jokes and comments must get wearing after the first couple of hundred times you hear them.

I prepare to dig in my heels and be dragged into early retirement.

Back at the gate the attendant announces. "There's an employee on board so we'll be removing him." They've just been playing with us. They must have known this all along.

We're running over an hour late when we finally take off. I'm in full fret mode now. Will my connection also be delayed? I console myself in the knowledge that it's far more serious for some of my fellow passengers. The lass sitting next to me is going to Singapore.

Getting off the plane is a drama. We pull up to the gate, but they can't connect the air bridge. The plane backs out and tries again. After some fiddling around, the air bridge is finally secured, but another 15 minutes have ticked away. Will I get a flight to Indianapolis today?

I go to the United rep at the gate. While we were in the air, they rebooked me onto the next flight. Which is due to board in 10 minutes. I've just about got time to walk to the gate. I'm reluctantly impressed by United's service.*

Why are there racing cars all over the airport? That's a bit weird. Then I twig. I'm in Indianapolis. They have some sort of car race here, I believe.

I worry about whether my back was redirected to my new flight. I needn't have. It soon pops out onto the carousel. A few minutes later I'm in a taxi heading towards my hotel.

Doesn't look too bad, Indianapolis. Not totally effed up like some cities. St. Louis had some wrecked streets. Not as bad as Detroit, but still pretty depressing. Can't spot any of that here. And look, they actually have some shops in the city centre.

Just before arriving at my hotel, I notice an enormous column. Judging by the date on it, I assume it's a Civil War memorial. And a pretty damn massive one.

I don't have long to rest in my hotel before this evening's event, which is quite a way out of the centre, in Broad Ripple. Not having eaten since breakfast, I need some food. Something simple, like a sandwich. I consult the computer and spot a sandwich shop, Pot Belly, just around the corner. It overlooks that huge column so isn't much of a challenge to find.

I quickly eat the sandwich back in my room. Roast beef, if you're interested. With lots of chili on the top. Nice and spicy.

"Can you call me a cab?" I ask at the hotel desk. "There should be one outside."

There indeed is. In fact there are several. I head towards the one at the front, but the drivers all start waving at me. It's not that one's turn, but the next to last one in the queue. Explain that system to me? How was I meant to guess that?

We head north but when we get close to our destination, my driver seems to get confused. He's overshot, but then has trouble finding his way back. He switches off the meter "I'll only charge you $20. That's the right fare." Very fair of him.

When we pull into Broad Ripple's car park, there's quite a crowd there. AS soon as I step out of the cab, one of the crowd comes up to me: "Hello, Ron." It's my contact here, Rick Burkhardt. He's a trim and active-looking retired police detective, with a beard that is in no way ironic.

At the bar, I'm introduced to the owner and founder, John Hill. His grey beard and musical northeast tones – still strong after 50 years in the USA – immediately conjures up my father. Who, like John, left his native Northeast as a young man. Except my father returned, John never did. Marrying, settling and eventually building his own pub, so he'd have somewhere to sit in his retirement.

I admire his long-term thinking. He also put in a brewery to make sure he could get the type of beer he likes to drink. It was the first brewery to open in Indiana for many decades.

I've ordered a cask ESB, but John warns me "Get something else. It's not ready yet. They've put it on too early. Have a Wobbly Bob."

I do. Though because they've run out of imperial pints, I get it in a 16 oz. glass.

John looks at my glass strangely, then explains: "It's named after my Dad. He could be a bit wobbly at times."

I spot a plate of scotch eggs being hurried to a customer. Now there's authentic for you.

There's a crowd of about 40 when I start to talk. Then it gets chilly. Someone goes inside and returns with a blanket to shelter under. The wind has picked up and the sheet functioning as a screen is flapping about like crazy. Slightly challenging circumstances. But I soldier through.

Once the questions are over, we adjourn inside out of the chill. Where I set up my impromptu book stall. I flog a good few books again. And sign some of mine people already own.

Bookselling done, I chat with Rita Kohn, legendary local beer writer. All I can say is that I hope I'm still as mentally sharp when I'm her age. Dolores already thinks my natural forgetfulness is the early onset of Alzheimer's.

I don't leave it too late. After eating my burger, Rick gives me a lift back to my hotel, along with his brother and a friend. We get talking about music and am surprised to find myself in the company of fellow punk fans. We talked punk all the way back to my hotel.

I don't have to be in bed too early tonight. Rick is picking me up in the early afternoon. I can rise whenever I please.

* They even sent me an email while I was airborne telling me about the rebooking.

A-06 Budweiser Brewhouse
Lambert International Airport

Potbelly Sandwich Shop
55 Monument Cir,
Indianapolis,
IN 46204.
Tel: +1 317-423-9043
https://www.potbelly.com/stores/23244

Broad Ripple Brewpub
842 E 65th St,
Indianapolis,
IN 46220, USA
Tel: +1 317-253-2739
http://www.broadripplebrewpub.com/

Speedway

As I promised myself, I rise fairly late. After a good, long, deep sleep. It's done me a power of good.

While I'm in the bathroom I hear a crash. The light next to the door has fallen down. I'm glad I wasn't standing underneath it at the time.

Having spotted a Rock Bottom brewpub just past that huge column, I trawl along there about noon. I'm not meeting Rick until 2 PM.

On the way, I take a good look at the monument. It commemorates Indiana citizens who fought in a whole series of wars, some obscure and some of which I haven't heard of. Most interesting is what isn't represented: WW I and WW II. I suspect the reason was that there was no space left.

They might not offer the most exciting beers in the world, but Rock Bottom brewpubs are pretty reliable, not stupidly priced and have OK food. Good enough for me. Especially as I plan on having a late breakfast here.

Mm. Don't really fancy any of the food for breakfast. I'll just have a double bourbon instead. Almost as nourishing as a fry up. I'm sure I'll be eating with Rick soon, anyway. What's the worst that could happen?

The footie is on the telly. And the Arses are getting whipped. Teehee.

Rick picks me up as arranged at 2 PM. Our first stop is at Daredevil. Which is out by the speedway. Which we go and take a quick look at.

The speedway is dead impressive. Mile-long stands, it looks like. Unfortunately, it's pissing it down again. I'm not getting out to take snaps. You'll have to look it up on the internet. I'm sure it has way better photos than I can take in this gloomy weather.

Daredevil is a cavernous modern space. Brewery one side, taproom the other. It's a pretty standard layout. That I'm seeing copied a lot in Europe.

We chat with Michael Pearson, head brewer and founder, and drink a couple of beers.

Before leaving, I'm given a couple of cans. That's a relief. I dare put these fuckers in my luggage. My faith in crown corks has been broken. And I'm sure those cans will come in handy, sometime*. When I don't fancy lugging a bottle along,

Next stop is Sun King. Who are fairly well-known, I hear, over here.

The weather hasn't improved. But the colourful muriel lifts my mood. Though really it's my stomach that needs lifting. I really should have had some breakfast. Still, what's the worst that could happen?

Excuse me if my brewery descriptions are turning to total crap. I've seen so many. Adored my reflection in so much stainless. I'm getting breweries out.

A brewers shows us around. But I'm feeling a little vague. We have eaten haven't we? I fear not. Still, these beers aren't that strong, are they?

Why am I lying on my bed fully clothed? Must have nodded off. I blame low blood sugar.

In the lobby I find an almost inedibly dry sandwich and a bag of crisps. Almost inedible. I manage to force it down.

At least they've fixed the busted light while I was out.

Where was it I had breakfast again?

* They do, indeed, come in handy.

Rock Bottom
10 W Washington St,
Indianapolis,
IN 46204.
Tel: +1 317-681-8180
http://www.rockbottom.com/locations/indianapolis-downtown

Daredevil Brewing
1151 N Main St,
Speedway,
IN 46224.
http://daredevilbeer.com/

Sun King Brewing
135 N College Ave,
Indianapolis,
IN 46202.
Tel: +1 317-602-3702
http://www.sunkingbrewing.com/

Crystal Lake

Another day of travelling ahead. Though not that complicated. Just a single flight to Chicago.

The taxi queue outside the hotel is as weird as yesterday. This time it's the turn of the rearmost taxi. I'm glad the drivers are keeping track. This time mine doesn't get lost. Though I guess the airport is pretty easy to find.

Checking in and security are a breeze once more. Why isn't it like this in European airports?

Sweets. I need to buy Alexei some sweets. Andrew gets bourbon, Alexei gets sweets. I see a spot selling just that. I get him two packets. What the fuck, $14! It shouldn't really be more than $4, the robbing bastards. I must remember not to shop in airports.

I need some food. Ah, there's a steakhouse. That'll do. As usual my arse is parked adjacent to the bar. I order a Sun King Osiris. And a steakburger. That should see me through the next few hours. I have to say that the beer choice is usually pretty good in US airports. Unlike most countries. (Wetherspoons in the UK being an exception.)

The woman behind the bar is quite pushy. She keeps asking everyone if they want more drinks. No thanks, missus. I'm happy just nursing this pint, thank you.

As I walk to my gate I pass a Granite City brewpub bar. Damn. I remember now noticing it when I flew in. I blame my poor whatdoyoucallit, that thingy. What is it? Memory, that's it.

Sadly, my United flight isn't overbooked. Looks like I'm condemned to more years of working.

Once again, I have little time to rest after my arrival in Chicago. I only have an hour or so before I need to be on a train to Crystal Lake, which is about 75 km northwest of the city centre. Why did I agree to do this event? Because they asked me. It's as simple as that.

It's my final event of the trip. I realise that I've only really had one free day.

I take a double-decker commuter train. It's pretty full, but I get a seat. Everyone but me is clearly on their way home after a day's work. My work is just beginning.

I'm trying to take a photo of the outside of Duke's Tavern, location of tonight's event, when someone pops out and say "Ron, we're in here."

After a second or two, I recognise who it is: Les Howarth. We met in Chicago last September. He takes me inside to meet some other members of his home brew club.

We start the evening with some food. Just as well, as it's hours since I last ate. Obviously accompanied by a beer or two. Once that's all out of the way we repair upstairs, where the meeting will take place. It's supposed to start at 19:00.

I have some equipment difficulties. There's no projector, just a large TV. And I don't have the right cable to connect by laptop up to it. They'll just have to make do with my laptop screen. Fortunately, it's not an enormous room.

There's beer to accompany me droning on. That's been the plan for most of my events. Me talking, home brewers serving historic Scottish beers. It's worked out pretty well, really.

I get a few laughs, which is usually a sign of things going well. But I can't linger too long afterwards. If I miss the 21:00 train I'll have to wait until 00:30 for the next one. Which would have me getting to bed far too late.

Once I've dumped all my stuff back in the hotel, I realise that I've still got a bit of a thirst. The internet tells me that there's a TGI Fridays a couple of blocks away. That'll do for a quick eye-closer. On my last night in the USA.

It doesn't have the greatest beer selection. I go for a Sam Adams Rebel. It does the job. I vaguely stare at the basketball on TV while I drink it. The trip is winding down. No more events, no more talking.

Just one place I need to drop by on my way to the airport tomorrow. Then I'm done. At least until the end of the month. When I'll be back in the USA again. This time for Asheville Beer Week.

Duke's Alehouse and Kitchen
110 N Main St,
Crystal Lake,
IL 60014.

Tel: +1 815-356-9980
http://thedukeabides.com

TGI Fridays
153 E Erie St,
Chicago,
IL 60611.
Hours: Open today · 10:30AM–2AM
Tel: +1 312-664-9820
https://www.tgifridays.com

Chicago

It's an indication of how full my schedule has been that even on my final day, I'm squeezing in a brewery visit. Literally on my way to the airport.

Goose Island, to be specific. I check out of my hotel and jump in a cab. There's a bit of buggering around at Fulton Market where a lorry is blocking the street. My driver tries to take a detour around it, but only finds a dead end. After a bit of messing around we get through.

Inside the brewery, Mike Siegel comes to greet me. He has Tyler of Present Tense with him. He just happened coincidentally to be in the brewery. Nice to see him again, too.

We go down to the pilot brewery to have a taste of the test run of our next collaboration beer. It's just about finished in primary, though still a bit yeasty. Still a bit rough around the edges, but some time in oak should knock those edges off.

I'm really interested in getting a look at the snapped brown malt Andrea Stanley has made for the project. The corns are very unevenly coloured, some near black others as pale as pale malt.

"Usually I'd reject malt that looked like that." Mike says. It does look a bit odd.

Mike can't stay with us long. He has a party to show around the brewery. He leaves us at the little bar area inside the brew house. We're free to pour whatever we fancy. So I get myself a Bourbon County Stout. "Why not?" I think.

Tyler and I have a pleasant chat about various things, including his brewery. Which still isn't properly up and running. A shame, because the cask of ESB he let us try in September was lovely stuff.

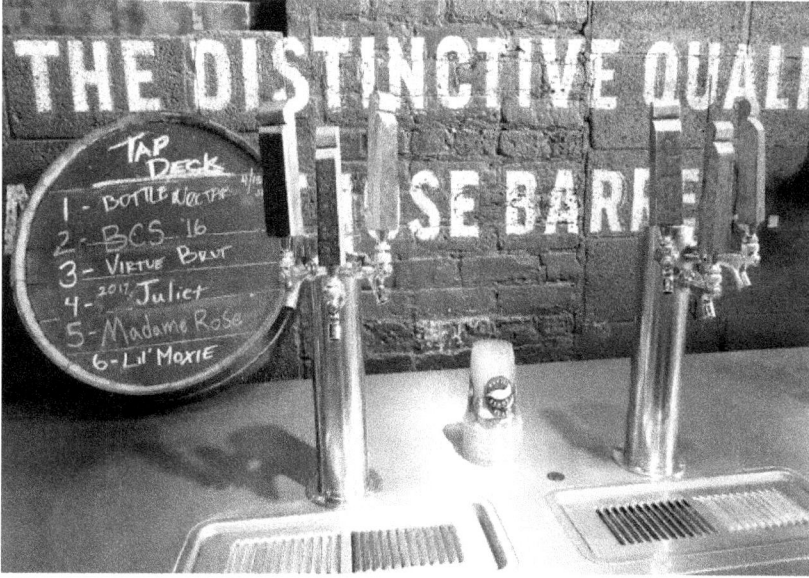

When Mike has finished showing his guests around he comes the bar for a chat. And gives me a few bottles to take home, as does Tyler. I love Mike's (literally) white label bottle which simply says in large letters "Not for resale". No worries on that count. I plan drinking it myself.

I can't stay too long. Got a transatlantic flight to catch. Soon another taxi is taking me along the concrete hell of the motorway to O'Hare.

I've a few tasks to accomplish. Like getting Andrew his bottle of Bourbon. And myself some food for the plane. I buy two sandwiches and it comes to almost $25. They aren't even that big or particularly good. Robbing bastards. I should remember not to shop in airports.

There's not much in the way of a bar in sight. So I make do with an Italian food place. Calamari and bourbon. That should set me up nicely for the flight.

Which it seems to do. I nod off nicely shortly into the flight, only to awake in Amsterdam with a yellow stain down the front of my shirt. Presumably from the dinner that was served.

The end of a really fun trip. Where once again I met loads and loads of people. Most of them pretty nice. Just three weeks and one day until I next cross the Atlantic. "You're crazy, Ronald." As Dolores always says.

Goose Island Beer Company
1800 W Fulton St,
Chicago,
IL 60612.
Tel: +1 800-466-7363
http://www.gooseisland.com/age-gate

http://presenttensefineales.com/

USA (part two)

Atlanta

As usual, the journey begins with a number 15 bus. All the way to Zuid this time, as the 197 doesn't currently stop at Haarlemmermeerstation.

It's an early start for me, as my flight is at 10:35. And they're still advising getting to Schiphol 3 hours before departure.

My heart sinks as I see the queue for the bag drop-off queue. Right out into the corridor. They're so busy that, in addition to the baggage machines, all the check in counters are manned. Which is where I drop off my bay, the old-fashioned way. At least I can see, as I wait to ditch my bag, that the security queue isn't all the way down the stairs this time.

The queue still isn't exactly what I'd describe as short. But bag drop-off, security and passport control only take an hour or so. Only? What's become of my expectations? Have they really got so low?

Once through all the shit, I pick up my traditional bottle of duty-free whisky. Not Laphroaig this time. I can't resist the Talisker at just €38.

On the way to my gate, I grab a bacon and egg sandwich. A classic health-food breakfast. Having plenty of time to kill, there's also time for a bar visit. I manage to resist Heineken Extra Cold and go for just normal Heineken. Which is still too cold for my tastes.

Once in my seat, I pug in the noise-cancelling headphones and look for shit comedy films to watch. I find the lightest sort of drivel makes the flight fly by. And that's what it's all about: making the journey seem as short as possible. And what's more drivelly than Neighbours 2? The sequel to a crap film.

Funnily enough, despite having visited Atlanta before, I've never been in the airport. Last time I arrived by train and left by Greyhound bus. Luckily, there isn't much of a queue for immigration. I'm through pretty quickly, but my bag is already on the carousel.

I'm staying downtown. Just for one night. I jump in a taxi to take me there. I'm pleased to learn that it's a fixed fare - $32. A bargain, considering how far out the airport is, compared to Schiphol.

I've arranged to meet Mitch Steele in the Porter Beer Bar at 6 PM. I'm a bit pushed for time and by the time my taxi drops me there, it's 6:15. But Mitch is nowhere to be seen. After a while I twig that I've set the time on my watch incorrectly. I actually arrived in the pub at 5:15.

I've plenty of time to check out the pub, a long thin affair. As usual, my arse is parked precariously on a bar stool.

Mitch duly trolls up at the appointed time. It's good to see him again. We always have dead interesting chats. This time, as so often, it turns to history. I express my fear that future historians will have very little hard information about the current crop of breweries. Mostly because brewers don't have brewing ledgers like in the old days. Electronic records, in particular, are likely to get lost.

http://hoptripper.com/brewing-records-and-why-they-matter/

We share a few beers, eat a little, but don't make it too late.

Back at my hotel, I force myself to stay awake another couple of hours. Watching some crap TV. When I do jump in bed, sleep comes quickly, emptying my overexcited mind like an unplugged sink.

The Porter Beer Bar
1156 Euclid Ave NE,
Atlanta,
GA 30307.
http://www.theporterbeerbar.com/

Asheville day one

I don't get the best night's sleep. Despite slipping into slumber easily. I wake around 4 AM and sleep fitfully thereafter.

I feel pretty knacked when I get up. A cooked breakfast. That's what I need to liven myself up. I make my way downstairs to the hotel restaurant. I start to order two eggs over easy and bacon, with coffee and orange juice.

The waitress tells me: "Getting the buffet breakfast will work out cheaper."

"OK, I'll have that then."

Having the buffet means I can pile extra bacon onto my plate. More bacon is never bad. The grease livens me up a bit. I return to my room for some lazing around watching TV. My flight to Asheville isn't until 13:10.

I'm through security in 5 minutes. Mind you, I do have TSA pre. Meaning I don't need to remove my watch, belt or shoes and my laptop can stay in its bag. I still don't understand why this is considered secure for TSA pre passengers, but not for everyone else. But I'm not complaining.

I must be tired. I can't be arsed to go to the bar. Instead I just wait at the gate reading Private Eye. As usual, they're overbooked and asking for volunteers to be bumped. Surely that just displaces the problem to the next flight, which is probably also overbooked?

It's only a small plane. Luckily I've only got a small rucksack as carry-on. I can just about squeeze it into the tiny overhead locker. Despite it weighing a ton, being packed with books. Just happy the damned thing is off my shoulder.

Mike Karnowski, owner, brewer and all-round dogsbody of Zebulon Artisan Ales, is picking me up. He has a sign saying "Dodgy Mild".

Once in his pickup, he pours me a beer from a vacuum flask. Into a full imperial pint glass.

"It's a 1920's AK. My all-day drinking beer. It's only 2.7%, so I can drink it while at work without getting smashed, but it still satisfies as a beer."

Very nice it is, too. Though he only brews it for himself. "It's too weak to sell commercially." I blame the US tax system – there's a flat rate of tax, irrespective of strength - for making lower-gravity beers unviable.

Before heading over to the brewery, we drop by the house where I'll be staying to drop off my junk. I'll have the whole place to myself, which is pretty cool. The owners – who live elsewhere – run their business from the basement. They only ask one thing of me: "Will you water the plant pots next to the front door every day? They get dry."

We chat with then a while then progress to Weaverville.

Weaverville, the location of his brewery, is a small town a few miles north of Asheville. A location in Asheville itself would have been too expensive, Mike explains.

On our way there, Mike tells me that he struggled to come up with a name for his brewery. The first few he came up with were too close to existing brewery names. With a few days to go until opening, he still hadn't settled on one. Then he came up with Zebulon.

"What does Zebulon mean?" I ask Mike.

"It's an old-fashioned southern first name."

A fictional planet in a 1950's Scifi novel is what popped into my head. I'm slightly disappointed by the real explanation.

This part of North Carolina is beautiful. Full of lushly wooded hills and rushing rivers. Though, obviously, this being the USA there's a motorway cutting right through them.

The brewery is in a former firehouse on an alleyway in the centre of Weaverville. Well, what there is of a centre. It's not a huge place. A couple of dozen businesses line Main Street.

A small area outside the brewery is roped off with a few barrels for tables and some chairs. Most of which are occupied. The entrance is through the front of a tardis, which Mike has borrowed for the occasion.

And what is that occasion? A recreation of the beers you'd find in an Edwardian pub. It's something I've dreamt of or years. In terms of beers, the years just before WW I are my favourites. When you'd find a decent range of strengths, colours and flavours. It's like travelling back in time to 1910. Hence entering via a tardis.

For $20, punters get a special glass and five smallish pours. Being a special guest, I get an imperial pint glass and as much beer as I can drink. Which, those who know me will attest, can be a frightening amount.

Gabe, Mike's partner, is on the door handing out the glasses and drink tickets.

These are the beers:

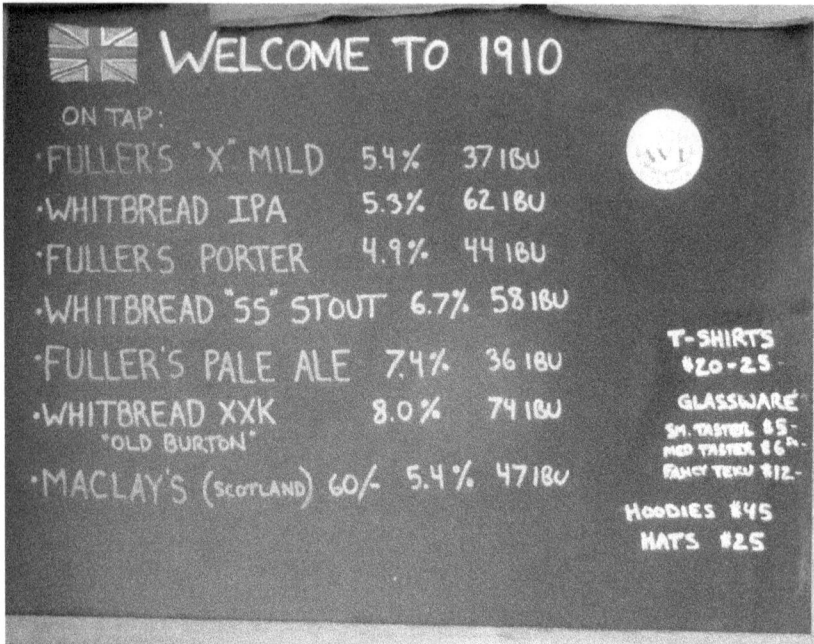

Chris, brewer at a small place in Asheville, is performing barman duties. Being sensible, I start with a Mild rather than a Burton. It's rather good. Not too sweet, but with a pleasant No. 3 invert character.

I'm soon chatting with various punters. Which is sort of what I'm here for. Surprising how many people know who the hell I am. Some mornings I'm not that sure. Several tell me that they saw my last talk. And are coming on Sunday. Can't have done that bad a job last time.

I shift a few books – which is sort of why I've come. I hope I can get rid of a lot more. It was a pain lugging as many over as I did. I want to return with as few as possible.

Explaining the beers, their history and ingredients is good fun. Always pleasant to not see eyes glazing over – as is the case with my family – when I talk about this stuff.

The stereo is blasting out a variety of 1970's punk classics. There's a reason for that. Connected with the talk I'll be giving on Sunday. But I'll get onto that later.

Browsing one of my books, young woman asks "What language is this? Is it Belgian?"

I take a look. Bum. I've brought over both my copies of the Dutch translation of the Home Brewer's Guide to Vintage Beer.

A young woman wearing muddied overalls enters. It's Chris's fiancée, Jessica. At first I think it's some bizarre fashion, like ripped jeans. Turns out that works on a farm and the mud spattering is genuine.

The brewery doesn't stay open late. The last punter is turfed out by 7 PM. Once everything is tidied up, we (Mike, Gabe, Chris, Jessica and I) move on to Hi Wire Brewing where there's a food truck.

I visited Hi Wire in the centre of Asheville last time I was in town. But that's not where we go. They've now got a second, much larger, location in Biltmore village, a little to the south of downtown.

We drink some more beer and I eat a Cuban sandwich. Which is a first for me.

We don't stay out that late. Which is just as well, me being well knackered. Sleep overtakes me quickly, like a BMW on the autobahn. Let's hope it doesn't end in a wreck again.

Zebulon Artisan Ales
8 Merchants Alley,
Weaverville,
NC 28787.
http://www.zebulonbrewing.com/

Hi-Wire Brewing - Big Top
2A Huntsman Pl,
Asheville,
NC 28803.
https://hiwirebrewing.com/big-top/

Asheville day two

Not the greatest sleep again. The latter half is a mix of dozing and restless turning.

The house I'm staying in has a hi-tech toilet. Though I'm too nervous to engage any of its special functions. They look a bit scary.

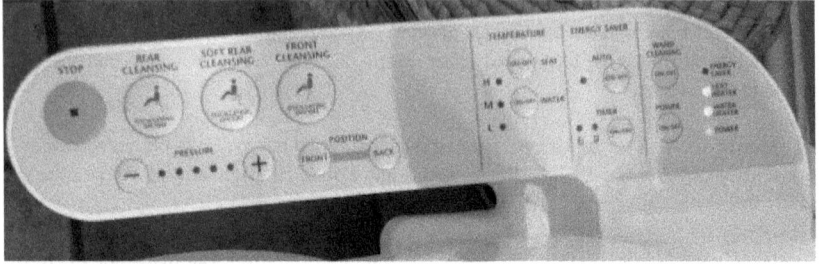

After warily completing my ablutions, I water the plant pots outside the front door. The garden is much nicer than the usual US expanse of bland lawn. It has plants and shit in it. Happy to keep it looking nice.

Mike picks me up at 10:30 and we drive over to the brewery in Weaverville. For the moment it's the brewery. Evidently another one is due to open soon just a little further down the same alleyway. For the record, Weaverville has a population of just 3,000. That's fewer inhabitants than Balderton, where I grew up. I can't imagine Baldo ever having two breweries.

On the way over, Mike tells me has no desire to get any bigger. His 7-barrel plant gives him total freedom to brew what he wants too. If he grew much bigger, then he wouldn't be able to experiment as much as he does. With no debt and no investors, he's in complete control. I'm sure it's a situation many brewers would envy.

I watch Mike set up, mop the floor, arrange the furniture outside and move the tardis into place. There's nothing quite as relaxing as watching someone else work while you have a beer in your hand. Especially when it's a full imperial pint. Not being a total pisshead, I kick off the day with Maclay 60 bob.

A beer that yesterday was confusing the hell out of the punters. Who expected a dark Scotch Ale and were served a beer above the same hue as Pils. It's a lovely light refreshing beer. Perfect for breakfast.

After a while, Gabe brings tacos. Which form the solid part of our breakfast.

Punk stuff is still spitting out of the speakers. Mike tells me he's been very impressed by The Damned. Not a band he'd known that well. I have to agree with him. Re-listening to them in preparation for this trip, I was pleasantly surprised by their musical prowess. Well put together songs, just played at kamikaze pace. You have to love a band that manages to get through a song in less than a minute.

Mike tells me about some frustrating customers:

"They come in and say: 'Give me your IPA.' When I say we don't have one, they turn around and walk out again. They drive all the way over here and then don't even bother having a beer."

At 1 PM Mike opens up and people start trickling in. The same scenario as yesterday: I tell people the background of the beers and try to flog books. While drinking from an imperial pint glass.

I didn't quite get around every beer yesterday. Putting that right is my first task. Starting with the Whitbread SS Stout.

The beers are going down well with the public. The Burton has been particularly well received. Though I'm pleasantly surprised by the popularity of the Mild. At least this one is the colour people expect a Mild to be: a darkish brown.

Maybe there is a place on today's bar far older, stronger forms of Mild. Stranger things have happened. Who the hell would have predicted Milk Stout making a comeback? A style as trendy as a fat fifty year old in a string vest a few years ago. Mind you, a string vest does feature in my talk tomorrow. A trendy one, too. The vest, I mean. Not my talk. They'll never be trendy.

A man around my age enters wearing a dog collar. Judging by the shoes and trousers he's wearing, I doubt very much that he's a vicar.

I have to agree with the punters: the Burton is very pleasant. And rather scarily easy-drinking. Getting totally plastered would be no problem. I'm ever more convinced my Edwardian pub idea would fly. Assuming there are other pissheads out there.

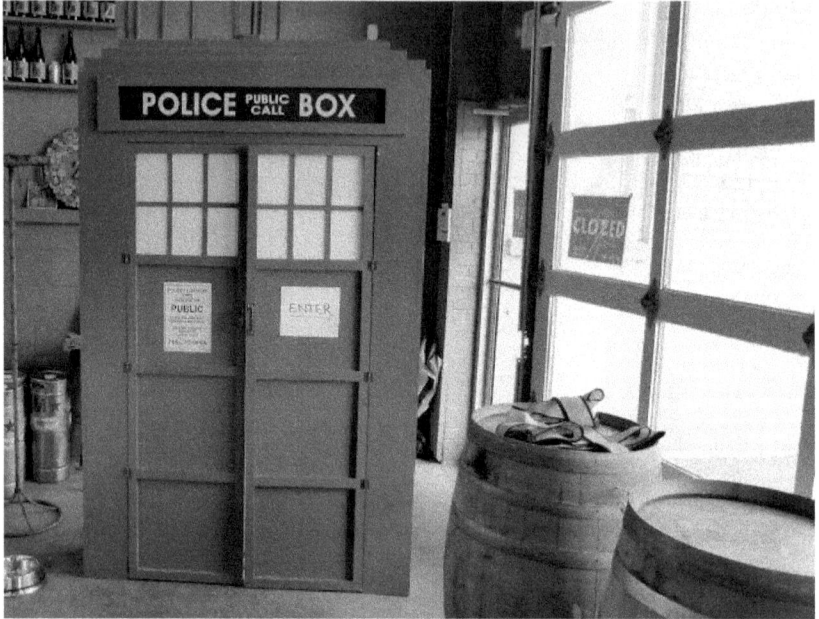

The concept is simple. Find a genuine Edwardian pub like, for example, the Adelphi or Garden Gate in Leeds, and have a range of Edwardian beers. Maybe occasionally jumping to another decade – say the 1930's – for a week. Please get in touch if you have a suitable pub and like the idea.

Mike seems to be shifting a fair number of the four packs of historic beer styles. Lost and Forgotten Beer Styles it's called. As is my talk tomorrow. The pack includes a little booklet which is a summary of that talk. An odd mix of beer history and punk reminiscences.

I ask Mike what connections the projector for tomorrow's talk has. "What projector? I plan using a whiteboard."

Ah, that's not great. "I've prepared a Powerpoint. I need a projector." Gabe puts out the word on social media to see if anyone has a projector we can borrow. I hate all the technical stuff.

Before I know it, closing time is upon us again. Mike, Gabe and I go to a pizza place. Only Gabe orders a pizza. Mike and I share a charcuterie plate, followed by sardines on toast.

Sitting outside with sausage evokes memories of lazy evenings in the Bavarian sticks, nibbling meat and cheese. Interrupted by languorous draughts of beer.

The light slips behind the hills and night creeps up to embrace us with its dark fingers.

Another good day.

Zebulon Artisan Ales
8 Merchants Alley,
Weaverville,
NC 28787.
http://www.zebulonbrewing.com/

All Souls Pizza
175 Clingman Ave,
Asheville,
NC 28801.
http://www.allsoulspizza.com/

Asheville day three

Not sure what's going on with the sleeping. The final half of the night is a checkerboard of waking and dozing. Leaving me not hugely refreshed.

I'm in no rush, at least. I'm not being picked up until around 3 PM. My plan is to wander into town and hit a couple of breweries.

I get an email from Mike asking what cables I have to connect my laptop to the projector. I've had problems with cables before and now always carry both an HDMI and a VGA one with me. I'm sure one will work.

Before leaving. I remember to water the flowerpots. It's been quite warm and I wouldn't want them drying out. It's the one thing my hosts requested. Wouldn't want to let them down.

The house isn't that far from South Slope, a neighbourhood in central Asheville with a stupid number of breweries. It's about a ten-minute walk. Pretty easy, especially as it's all downhill. But there's the long-term problem: the walk back is all uphill. Up a pretty steep hill. And, after my decades residing in the Netherlands, I'm all out of hill-climbing capacity.

I decide to start out at Green Man. Their new place, which was half-built last time I was in town. The brewery, the old one, where Mike used to work.

It's a beautiful, sunny day as I work my way down the hill. Through an archetypal neighbourhood of wood-clad houses, embraced by mature trees and proper gardens, not just the usual lawns. (The steepness of the land rules out lawns of any size.) Like a film set of the idyllic American street.

At the bottom of the hill is a weird pub we noticed last night. It still has the signs up for a tool shop, but inside is a strange Hawaiian sort of place*.

The new Green Man building is huge. The downstairs bar is at least two normal storeys high. Looks like it cost a few bob. Though it is a bit cavernous. And lacking atmosphere.

Flagship ESB 5.5%
Looks too dark to me – more like a Brown Ale. Tastes too roasty. And a bit on the sweet side. Given it blind, I would never have guessed it was an ESB. Apart from the ABV, it doesn't seem to have much in common with the Fullers beer.

The barmaid just gave me a taster of Berry Berlinerwiesse (it really is spelt "wiesse"). Not very sour and with an artificial-tasting fruit flavour. More like an alcopop than a Berliner Weisse.

I did reasonably well flogging books yesterday – eight in total. Hopefully I can shift the remaining 25 today.

Quite a few people have wanted to have their photo taken with me. Which is slightly weird. Odd that I seem better known on this side of the Atlantic.

Time for another beer.

Trickster IPA 6.4% ABV
A bit hazy, but not full-blown murk. Nice tropical fruit aroma – mango, passion fruit, peach. (I know that last one isn't tropical). A pleasant enough IPA.

Most people are going upstairs to the patio. Presumably to bake themselves in the sun. No way I'll do that. I like to maintain my healthy pallor.

Everyone under 30 is being asked to show ID. Why didn't they ask me? I still look like I'm under 30, don't I? I do in my head. Surely that's what everyone else sees, too?

Two is enough for here. I feel like checking out Wicked Weed. Just to see if I can taste the evil in their beer yet.

It's pretty hot outside. I work up a nice sweat walking up the slight incline to Wicked Weed. That big hill on the way back to the house is going to be fun. But that's later.

The takeover doesn't seem to have put folks off. The patio is mobbed. As is the bar inside. Luckily, there are two free seats. But before I can grab one, two women move in. Though they don't sit down. Obviously they're just going to order. So I hover behind them until they're done. Amazingly, the barmaid ignores them and asks me if a want to order, despite me standing well back from the bar.

Eventually the women are done and I can park my sorry fat arse at the bar.

BA Smoked Rye, 8.5% ABV ($5.75 for a snifter)
Big and Stouty. Thankfully not too smoky.

Evidently no-one has heard how wicked this brewery now is. Then again, quite a few people are ordering house Chardonnay. So not exactly beer geeks.

The slightly drunk young man sitting next to me asks if I'm writing beer reviews. "Just taking notes to I can remember what I've drunk." I reply. A bit later he's led away by his very pregnant wife. Must be a fun day watching hubby get pissed while drinking water.

I order a roast beef sandwich. Got to eat sometime.

Not tasting the evil in the beer yet. Maybe it was brewed before the sellout. I get another beer, too:

Pernicious IPA, 7.4% ($4.75 for a US pint)
It's pretty cheap in here, really. A grapefruity IPA. Quite bitter for a modern US IPA. Pretty easy drinking, though.

The nice young people from NYC sitting next to me wonder which King Henry has his face on the wall. "Is it Henry V or Henry VI?"

"It's Henry VIII," I tell them, "the one with all the wives. He never said that about hops, you know. He only forbade Ale brewers from using hops. He had his own personal Beer brewer, who did brew with hops."

Hope that didn't come across as too pushy. They continue to chat with me, so I guess not.

I deliberately leave returning until quite late. I'm hoping that Gabe, who's picking me up, will arrive before I get to the top of the hill. I really don't fancy the climb. I've only gone about 50 metres up the hill when I hear a car horn behind me. It's Gabe. Now how's that for timing?

The man who wore the dog collar yesterday is here. Totally civilian dressed. Knew he was no vicar. Eventually.

The brewery is filled with chairs. Around 50 or so. After 4 PM those with VIP tickets start rolling up. It entitles them to a chat with me before the crowd turns up. Which is what happens. I also shift a couple of books, which is always good.

I've brought a selection with me. The home Brewer's Guide to Vintage Beer. Both volumes of Scotland!. And a few copies of Mild!, Strong! And Porter!. There are quite a few of my books clogging up our living room. Dolores would love to see the back of them.

Mike has jerry-rigged a screen from two boards. It's held up with duct tape, but keeps falling down. I connect my laptop to the projector using the HDMI cable. Nothing appears on the screen. Oh no. I fiddle with the video output key. Still nothing. Someone hands me the projector manual. Looks like I need to connect using VGA. Thankfully, that works.

That's a relief. I feel naked when there are no pretty pictures behind me.

Mike is my warm-up act. He gives a talk – using a marker and big sheets of paper, which he hangs up - comparing Old English 800, a Malt Liquor, to an 1880's X Ale. The specs are surprisingly similar, except for the hopping rate. He provides tasters of both the Malt Liquor and an X Ale he's brewed himself. It's a wonderfully bonkers concept.

Then it's my turn. Being a new talk, I've a few jitters. Including stuff on music, which I've never talked about (in public) before.

Half of the screen keeps falling down. But it doesn't put me off my stride. Eventually we just prop it up.

Based on the number of laughs I get (my usual maatstaaf (apologies for the Dutch. It's the first word that came into my head. Sometimes I think my inburgering has been too successful)) it goes really well. And there are lots of questions. A surprisingly large number about the music part.

Questions done, I hang around a while to chat. Then Mike, Gabe and I head out to eat. A pizza place again. Where I again don't eat pizza.

* Looking it up on the internet, it's a place selling kava, a drink made from a root grown on pacific islands, which seems to have some mild psychoactive effect.

Noble Kava
283 Biltmore Ave,
Asheville,
NC 28801.
http://www.noblekava.com/

Green Man Brewery
27 Buxton Ave,
Asheville,
NC 28801.
http://www.greenmanbrewery.com/

Wicked Weed Brewing Pub
91 Biltmore Ave,
Asheville,
NC 28801.
http://wickedweedbrewing.com/

Zebulon Artisan Ales
8 Merchants Alley,
Weaverville,
NC 28787.
http://www.zebulonbrewing.com/

Atlanta again

Another fairly restless night. What's wrong? I'm usually such a good sleeper.

Mike has given me a four pack of the beers from last night's talk. After my bad experience with beer-soaked clothes on my last US trip, I'm a bit wary of having bottles in my checked-in bag. Especially corked and caged ones.

I drink the Cotbusser and Grodziskie. Seeing the level of carbonation in them, it's a wise choice, I feel. Both are good beers. And, not being too strong, make the perfect breakfast.

Did I mention how good a brewer Mike is? Mild, AK, Burton – he can brew all the important styles well.

Mike is giving me a lift to the airport. He's picking me up a couple of hours early so we can drop by Sierra Nevada. It's right next to the airport, so why not?

The Sierra Nevada complex is enormous. After passing the ornate gates monogrammed "SN", it's a half mile or so to the brewery itself. Which is also pretty big. As is the parking lot. And the shiny copper kettles I can glimpse through the windows. They look about the same size as those in the old Heineken brewery in Amsterdam.

The tap room, obviously, is huge. And full. We find seats in one corner. A prime spot, next to the bogs. Unfortunately, the collaboration beer with Fullers, which was on cask, is all gone. Bit of a bummer that. I have an IPA of some sort instead.

We order food and chat. Neither of us get large meals. I have some delicious pork belly. Yummee!

I finish with a Bigfoot. Which I've only ever had bottled until now.

Mike drops me at Asheville airport and we say our goodbyes. It's been great spending time with Mike again. A talented brewers and all-round good bloke.

Being a tiny airport, the formalities take next to no time. But, being a tiny airport, there's only one bar. And all the seats at it are occupied. I go to the gate instead and read Private Eye.

Bad weather in Atlanta means nothing is allowed to take off or land. Which delays my flight by 30 to 40 minutes. No biggie for me. I've nothing planned this evening. And no connecting flight. Unlike most of my fellow passengers, who are looking a little nervous.

They're asking for bump volunteers again. Starting offer is 400 Delta dollars. When they raise it to $600, a woman close to me accepts. Her daughter is a bit miffed. "I'll have to hang around at Atlanta airport waiting for your flight."

It's a bigger aircraft this time. Much larger overhead bins. Though me rucksack is much lighter since I got rid of most of the books it carried.

I'm staying at a different hotel from the one on my way in. Though it's only about 50 metres away. The lifts are really weird. One set takes you up two floors. Then you have to walk around the corner to a second set that takes you to higher floors. A bit of a pain.

I mooch around my room for a while, watching some crap TV. And a little baseball.

There's been a spectacular fight. Giants pitcher Hunter Strickland pinged the hip of National's Bryce Hunter with a fastball. He saw it as deliberate, ran over to the mound and tried to whallop the pitcher. Neither looked a very accomplished fighter. Like two kangaroos boxing. It ended up with all the players from both sides piling in. There are endless replays from all possible angles.

My destination this evening is Max Lager's brewpub, just a couple of hundred yards down Peachtree. They claim it's Georgia's oldest brewpub. Who am I to doubt them?

Bit gloomy and not very full. Maybe everyone is upstairs where there are more draughts (but a smaller food offering). Me and yet another bar make acquaintance. Soon it gets pretty intimate. As intimate as a bar and a belly can be.

What should I drink? Not another IPA. I know – a Porter.

Three Threads Porter, 5.8% ABV
Oh no, that Three Threads shit again. Nice and dark. Decent coffee/cocoa flavour. OK.

The only other people at the bar are a couple speaking Polish and a man in his mid-50's shovelling food down while going tippy-tap on his phone. He occasionally comes up for air and orders a beer. This is fun.

The Polish couple keep staring, not exactly at me, more around me. They seem fascinated by something behind me. Presumably fellow diners. I really don't feel like turning around and looking. Partly from my English desire to avoid any possible embarrassment. Partly because I'm totally knacked and really can't be arsed.

I can barely force myself to knock back the beer. But I do. And a not too inspiring hamburger.

Just the one beer. And the last two bottles from Mike back in my room. The strong two, October Beer and Arctic Ale. They soon sentence me to slumbering.

Sierra Nevada Brewing Co.
100 Sierra Nevada Way,
Fletcher,
NC 28732.
http://www.sierranevada.com/

Max Lager's Wood-Fired Grill & Brewery
320 Peachtree St NE,
Atlanta,
GA 30308.
http://www.maxlagersrestaurantatlanta.com/

Leaving Atlanta

No need to rise too early. Not much to do this morning other than pack. And watch some shit TV.

My plan is simple: check out at noon, wander down street to pub, drink beer. It is pretty much my plan for every day. Eat some food. That would be a good idea, too.

Having flogged a reasonable number of books, my luggage is lighter. Most of the remaining books I load into my check-in bag. Leaving the bits I'm going to be carrying much lighter. Hooray.

I check out and leave my bags at the hotel. Then make the sort walk to Meehan's. As you might have guessed from the name, it's an Irish pub. But I know they have a reasonable beer selection. I was here a couple of years ago. I can't be arsed to trek any further.

I wedge myself betwixt stool and bar counter and order a beer.

Terrapin Hopsecutioner IPA, 7.3% ABV
Pale and fairly clear. Pretty grapefruity, but not that bitter, really. A pleasant enough lunchtime beer.

Not feeling quite so knacked today. Though I'm still a bit yawny. It's been an odd trip. Just five nights and a single event. That that did go really well.

Oh no, there's an advert for Golden Corral on the TV. What bad memories that recalls. Makes me literally want to vomit.

The barman just gave me a taster of Orpheus Transmigration of Souls, a Double IPA of 10%. Hides the booze very well.

They keep showing the baseball brawl from yesterday. Odd that two big strong athletes should fight like 8-year-old wimps.

I'm wondering what to eat. I'm tempted by fish and chips or shepherd's pie. But both are more than I really want to eat. I spot a bloke along the bar tucking into tacos. Hadn't noticed then on the menu. Looks perfect. I order them.

They're pretty damn good. And not too heavy. My stomach is always like Andrew's when I'm in the US.

For some reason there are Liverpool scarves behind the bar. Not from Liverpool itself, but all sorts of US Liverpool supporters' clubs. Maybe it's the Irish/catholic connection.

Time for another beer.

Orpheus Transmigration of Souls, 10% ABV

An Atlanta beer, evidently. Bit cloudier, this one. More of an Izal taste here – is that Citra? Or is it Simcoe? One of those weird modern hops. OK, I guess. Again, not that bitter. What's happening to US IPA? Has it turned into a sort of fruit punch?

It's not that busy. The staff chatting and joking with each other. Pretty friendly. I suppose it is a wet Tuesday lunchtime. Not exactly peak pub time.

Odd thing about my talk yesterday was that I got almost as many questions about music as beer.

It's so strange when I'm "on stage". I feel really confident, have all these jokes come into my head, can cope with anything that goes wrong, never run out of words to say. Almost like I'm a different person. Getting a whole room to laugh out loud is quite a rush. I can understand why people get addicted to performing.

I'm such a lucky bastard. I get to travel all over. Meet lots of cool people. And even get some of it paid for. If only I were 20 years younger. I reckon I've got another ten years more of this. Then the travelling will start getting too hard. Though Mum made it to Australia when she was 74.

Just saw the Tetley sign again on the way to the bogs. God, that brings up mixed emotions.

Three pints of DIPA. That should do me for today. No expensive airport whisky necessary.

Oh no, Golden Corral on the TV again. Excuse me while I go for a puke in the bog.

Bill paid, back picked up and taxi hailed, I'm on my way to the airport through a dark and rainy Atlanta. A city I've still seen bugger all of, despite a couple of visits.

My bag is soon checked in and I'm breezing through security. I love having TSA pre. It save so much bother. And undressing.

I always try to eat some decent food before a transatlantic flight. Great, there's a food court. Usually that means good value. I go to a Chinesey place and order Peking beef (no rice) and two spring rolls. It's not really spicy, but pretty tasty. So much so, that I fetch another. It's only $3 something a pop. Bargain.

I've still got some time before boarding. Why not drop by that TGI Fridays over there? I squeeze into a barstool. And order a Sweetwater 420 Extra Pale Ale. And a double bourbon.

After watching a couple of crap films, I get my head down. I manage to get a couple of hours of reasonable sleep. Not that much worse than most nights while I was away.

My bag is the third off. Great. Time to get a taxi.

Meehan's Public House Downtown
200 Peachtree Street,
Atlanta,
GA 30303.
http://meehanspublichouse.com/location/downtown

Scotland

Macbeth comes to Edinburgh

I rise early. Even earlier than for work. My flight being at 9:20, I need to be in the airport for 7:20.

At least that's what Schiphol is still advising. Get there two hours in advance (three hours for intercontinental flights) if you want to be sure of making your flight. After some recent experiences at Schiphol, I'm taking no chances.

Last time here, after having queued up for 30 minutes, I was told while checking in that I could have used the priority lane. So I give it a whirl. No problems. I'm in the much shorter priority queue for security. I'm through in ten minutes, including the traditional extra inspection of my trolley bag. It always gets pulled out, for some reason.

My flight departs from pier D. And I've plenty of time. Time a plenty to drop by the Irish pub for a quick Murphy's Stout and Jamesons whiskey. I also pick up a bacon and egg sandwich, which I eat on my way to the pub. It's my breakfast.

The flight is, thankfully, uneventful. And on time. About.

It's not far to my hotel. I'm stopping out at the airport as it was so effing extortionate in the city centre. And it still wasn't cheap here. It's long before the official check-in time of 3pm when I troll up. But I can go to my room straight away. Which is great. I had been worrying that I'd need to leave my bags, head off into town, then return to move everything to my room.

After a bit of arranging shit – mostly switching on my laptop and accessing the internet - I take the tram into town. I've got quite a bit of shit with me for this evening's talk: laptop and a dozen or so books I'm hoping to flog.

I start at the Playfair, a Wetherspoons in a shopping centre. Why? Because it's close to where the tram terminates. And I want to get some cheap food inside me. I'm not made of effing money. And I need plenty of ballast for a long day.

Soon I'm happily sat behind a pint and an all day brunch. I'm not at the bar, but at a high table. Why? There are no seats at the bar in Wetherspoons. The eggs aren't very well cooked. The yokes are hard. Oh well. There's no toast to mop it up, anyway.

The place is full of the usual odd mixture that you find in Wetherspoons. Grannies drinking tea, grandads drinking John Smiths Smooth, two women of indeterminate age tapping on their phones in front of half pints of white wine, a young couple eating, daytime drinkers knocking back pint after pint of Lager. And me. Not sure which type of customer I count as.

I don't linger that long. Things to do, beer to drink. I'm headed over to the Old Town. Which, given it's a bit of an uphill trek, isn't much fun with the rucksack full of books on my back.

My destination is the Jolly Judge. It's down an alleyway and I manage to walk past it. Meaning extra unnecessary uphill walking. That's not fun at all.

The castle and the higher parts of the Old Town hide behind a smokescreen of mist. When I reach the top, it's like walking into a cloud.

It's not a huge pub, but I manage to find a seat. And am soon tucking into a pint. A middle-aged couple comes and sits next to me. I hear that they're speaking Dutch to each other. The woman asks me: "Are you a local or another tourist?" "Ik ben ook een toerist." I reply. We proceed to have a long conversation in Dutch. Which is pretty strange.

They've McEwans 70/- and 80/- on keg. I thought the shilling names were usually reserved for cask. Weird to think that those two beers used to be dead common.

I have a couple, then move on. I don't want to be too late at the Hanging Bat. The location of tonight's talk. It kicks off at 7pm, but I aim to get there by six. I don't quite make that time. Doesn't matter so much as there's not really anything to set up.

Johnny Horn, the brewer here, recognises me as soon as I walk through the door. He thrusts a beer into my grateful hand and guides me downstairs, where all the action will happen. It's not a huge space, with room for an audience of 20-odd. And no projector. Hence the lack of setting up.

Four William Younger beers are served as I blab:

> 1851 60 shilling ale (6%)
> 1851 80 shilling ale (7.5%)
> 1851 stock ale (8.5%)
> 1885 140 shilling ale (9.5%)

It's a bit odd, being the only one who can see all the pretty pictures of my Powerpoint. Not much point going discussing tables of numbers in detail when no-one can see them but me. Rather surreal. I hope it hasn't detracted too much from the magic of hearing me speak.

Allan McLean, who I've never met before, and Robbie Pickering, who I have, are in the audience. We have a chat. I'll be seeing Robbie again tomorrow in Glasgow.

I only sell two books. The bag of books I lug back to the tram stop is almost as heavy as before. And there's still a hill to climb.

I don't stay up too late. I need to be up fairly early tomorrow to travel to Glasgow for my date at the Scottish Brewing Archive. It's going to be a very busy day.

The Playfair
Omni Centre
Leith Street
Edinburgh EH1 3AJ

Jolly Judge
493 Lawnmarket,
Edinburgh EH1 2PB.
http://www.jollyjudge.co.uk/

The Hanging Bat
133 Lothian Road
Edinburgh
City of Edinburgh EH3 9AB
http://www.thehangingbat.com/

Macbeth comes to Glasgow

I'm a bit later at Waverley Station than I'd hoped. Missing the 9:30 train to Glasgow I'd planned to take. It doesn't help that the nearest tram stop is quite a walk from the station.

But the next train is only 15 minutes later. Meaning I have time to buy two bacon baps. They'll be my breakfast. On the train.

I forgot to buy a drink to accompany my salted grease. Luckily there's a chirpy young man with a trolley and I can get myself a cup of tea to wash the food time.

This is a new train route for me. And, for the most part, a very attractive one, through verdant pastures bounded by craggy hills. It's all very green. Then again, it is raining. And looks like it has been for the last couple of hundred years.

It's a short hop on the subway from Queen Street Station to Kelvinhall, closest stop to the Scottish Brewing Archive. They seem to have poshed the subway stations up. Though there is still that strange smell down on the platforms.

The archive's surroundings have changed quite a bit. The flour mill has been replaced by student flats. Which probably explains all the young Chinese women on the streets on my way here.

I've requested 34 documents. Should keep me busy for most of the day. The nice young lady who is the archivist today already has the first batch ready. I've six hours to get through them all. Meaning I've got fewer than ten minutes per document. Plenty. I hope.

While I'm busy with my snapping marathon a few students trickle in and out. Mostly young women, who look at a few documents, photographing them on their phones and making notes. All in a leisurely way, unhurried way. I barely notice, busy as I am hacking rocks from the coal face.

At 13:30 I'm through everything they've brought up. "The next lot will be here around two." The nice young lady says. I retreat to the lounge for a glass of water and a read of a history magazine. Then at two, I get out my pickaxe again.

I feel quite sorry for the archivist when TU/6/9/1 appears. It's a loose-leaf brewing book that's almost the same size as her. And is probably heavier. I can barely lift the thing.

As usual, I don't waste much time studying the documents. Just photograph them and move on to the next. Some are notebooks where I need to snap every page. Others are brewing book where just a few sample pages will suffice.

I'm surprised when at 16:00 the nice young lady says: "That's the last one." But also happy, despite my aching back and blackened fingers. I've taken 1,476 photos in 5 hours. 4.5 hours if you allow for my break. Not bad going at all. Though it will take me months to process everything.

I'm meeting Robbie Pickering in the Three Judges ad 17:00. I get there pretty early – 16:15. I can barely get through the door. There some sort of do on. Is it a wake? Lots of people are wearing black. I wriggle my way to the bar and get myself a pint.

I eventually find a seat in a corner and read the paper and occasionally sip my beer. It's very soothing.

Robbie turns up half an hour later. He comes over with two pints of Loch Lomond Stout, one for each of us. "You look like you need a beer." He explains.

It's a lovely beer, bible black and beautifully burnt. So nice, that I go to the bar and buy two more pints.

The landlady comes by and says we're welcome to help ourselves to sandwiches from the buffet. Thee wake, or whatever it was, hasn't got through all their food. I tuck in enthusiastically.

"Do you fancy a pint of Bass?" Robbie asks. "Oh, yes, please. Not had it for ages."

I let him lead the way. He knows this part of Glasgow well. We're headed to Tennents. When I first spot the sign, I assume it's the brewery name. It isn't. It really is the name of the pub. Evidently it used to be run by someone called Tennent. And yes, he was related to the brewing family.

It's pretty crowded in here, too. Robbie comes back with two lovely looking pints.

I take a large draught of my Bass. Where's the farty smell? I wonder. It's not a bad pint. Just doesn't really taste like Bass.

"Do you want to try mine?" Robbie enquires. I'd assumed we both had Bass. Our pints look much the same, but his is Marstons Pedigree. They taste pretty different, mind. The Bass being much drier.

With no seat in sight, vertical drinking it is. The last thing I want, more standing. I've been on my feet most of the day. I'm not 18 any more. Nor 50, which I'd take, given the offer. I'm just thankful I can still stand unaided.

"What about a curry?" You don't have to ask me that twice. Especially as eating a curry pretty much guarantees sitting down. We go to Ashoka, which is just around the corner.

They have some interesting cross-cultural items on the menu. Like Haggis Pakora. "It's better than it sounds." Robbie assures me. He's right. Even if it is rather odd.

I order Pardesi Paneer and a nan. Both are pretty good, though the curry could have been hotter. I wish I'd known earlier about the curry. I wouldn't have been so gungho with the sarnies.

After we've eaten, I head back to Queen Street Station on the subway. I don't want to get back too late.

Entering the concourse, I swim against the stream of girls in miniskirts and makeup, in town for a big Friday night out. A cheering sight, youngsters in search of fun. All I'm looking for right now is the quickest route to my bed.

I leave the train at Haymarket. It's closer to the airport than Waverley. And the tram stop is right next to the station.

I'm in bed by 22:00. Though tomorrow is a totally free day. Nothing to do, other than find a pub where I can watch Scotland play England without getting killed.

Three Judges
141 Dumbarton Road,
Partick, Glasgow G11 6PR.

Tennent's Bar
191 Byres Rd,
Glasgow G12 8TN, UK
https://www.thetennentsbarglasgow.co.uk/

Ashoka Ashton Lane
19 Ashton Ln,
Glasgow G12 8SJ, UK
http://www.ashokaashtonlane.com/

Macbeth comes back to Edinburgh

I have a bit of a lie in. I hung out the do not disturb sign last night. No chance of a chambermaid bumbling in on me in my underscuds.

It's almost noon when I pull myself away from the TV and head on to the tram stop. Did I mention that my hotel is just far enough away from the airport for the walk to be annoying?

In town, I get a sudden craving for a bacon butty. Oh look, there's a Greggs. "A bacon sandwich, please." "Sorry, we don't do those after eleven." You what? That's just crazy. Especially at the weekend. My bacon craving is unfulfilled. At least for the moment.

I amble towards the city centre along Princes Street. Until I get to Frederick Street, where I make a left. Not randomly. Oh, no. I have a plan. Actually, not that different from Thursday's plan. I plan dining in style again. At the other city centre Wetherspoons, The Standing Order.

Inside, it's more like standing room only. I'm on my second round of the rooms when I finally find a seat. I stick my coat on a chair and head to the bar. Where I order the strongest beer on offer and an all-day brunch.

Wooha IPA, 6.2% ABV, £3.19
Unfined, it says on the pump clip, which explains the haze. At least it isn't total murk. It's the grapefruit juice sort of IPA, not that bitter, mind. Pleasant enough and reasonably strong.

I'm totally free today, so I'll just be slowly walking around town and doing a little light shopping. Then find a pub where I can watch Scotland England without getting killed.

The brunch is much better today. More nicely presented and the yolks are runny.

Good day at the Scottish Brewing Archive yesterday. I took almost 1500 photographs in five hours. Not sure the Majority Ale book has much useful in it, really. Though I'm dead excited about the notebook of the Copenhagen trip. And the Usher's records of the 1960's and 1970's. The late Younger's records, on the other hand, were a bit rubbish, with almost nothing filled in. I'll be busy for weeks – if not months – going through it all.

Thornbridge Jaipur, 5.9%, £3.10
Thought I'd play relatively safe. Quite bitter. And twiggy hop flavoured. Tastes different to how I remember ii. Less fruity. Much more English tasting than I expected.

Three middle-aged Scottish women sitting on the next table are discussing food. "I don't like feta cheese." "I do like couscous." "How can you be bothered to boil an egg every morning?"

Scotland are playing Italy at rugby. Where is it? It looks rather hot. And the stadium isn't that full. Ah, it's Singapore. Why the hell are they playing there?

I only stay for the two. I fancy a couple in the Abbotsford, down at the end of Rose Street. On the way down I notice they're putting up an England flag in the window of a pub. Could be a good spot to watch the game later.

The Abbotsford is looking as gorgeous as ever. I take a seat at the bar.

Windswept Wolf, 6% ABV, £4.40
Looks lovely: black with a tight, cream-coloured head. Served through a tall font. Dark and Strong Scottish Ale it's billed as. Sweetish and malty. It makes a nice change of pace.

Impressive array of malts above the pot shelf. Which seem to be arranged alphabetically: Aberlour, Ardbeg, Arran, Auchentoshan, etc.

This is a proper pub. Just the sound of conversation. There's a classic Scottish island bar. Odd that they have five tall fonts and one handpull. Maybe that's for English beer. All those on tall fonts are Scottish.

Where will I watch the game? If the worst comes to the worst, I can always go back to the Wetherspoons. They have a big screen there.

No-one but me seems to be drinking the cask. Most punters are ordering Tennent's.

Orkney Blast, 6% ABV
Billed as an IPA Barleywine hybrid. I've no effing idea what that means. And writing Barley
Wine as one word really isn't on this side of the Atlantic. Pretty pale and pretty clear. Apart
from the fizzing, not that unlike a pint of Tennent's the bloke to my right is supping. A US
hop thing going on, but also a sticky malt sweetness. Not getting the IPA bit. More like a
lower ABV Barley Wine. Quite nice, mind, and full of the alcoholy umph I like.

Time to watch the footy. I make my way back down Rose Street to Milnes. The pub where
I'd seen them putting up the England flag. It's very crowded, but I manage to squeeze my
way to the bar to get a pint, then squeeze my way to a spot where I can see a TV. I've got the
time mixed up and the first half is already 20 minutes in.

England are in control, but not really looking like scoring. Everyone in the pub gets very
excited on the rare occasions Scotland get anywhere near England's goal. It's scoreless at
half time. The second half is much like the first, with England knocking the ball around fairly
harmlessly.

Bum. England are bringing on Oxlade-Chamberlain. One of those Arsenal lightweight
forwards who always look out of their depth at the highest level. Why the hell did they bring
him on? He must have heard my thoughts, because he wriggles past several defenders and
sticks the ball past the goalkeeper. Bastard. Just trying to prove me wrong. I manage to
contain my emotions and show no outward sign of joy.

England look like they're coasting to a win. Just 10 minutes to go. Until they give away a free kick just outside the penalty box. The bastard Scot who takes it curves the ball around the wall and into the top right corner. Everyone in the pub goes mental. Except me. Bastards.

A couple of minutes later England give away another free kick in an even better position. This time the ball goes in the top left corner. The sound in the pub is totally deafening. Everyone is going totally apeshit. Except me.

As the final minutes of the game tick by, it looks like England are stuffed. Then, with virtually the last kick of the game, Harry Kane coolly sidefoots a cross into the bottom corner. Everyone in the pub is totally silent. Except me. I've been so resolved to England effing it up, that I can't contain a little yelp of joy. No the best idea in the circumstances.

Luckily, everyone is too busy crying into their beer to have noticed. I finish my pint and leave before anyone comes to their senses.

I make it an early night. I can't cope with any more excitement. I watch England play Argentina at rugby somewhere in the Andean foothills. England score a try with just seconds to go to win the game. Seems a recurring theme today.

The Standing Order
62-66 George St
Edinburgh,
Midlothian EH2 2LR.
Wetherspoon's.

Abbotsford Bar & Restaurant
3-5 Rose Street, Edinburgh,
Midlothian EH2 2PR.
+44 131 225 5276
http://theabbotsford.com/

Milnes of Rose Street
21-25 Rose St,
Edinburgh EH2 2PR.
Tel: +44 131 225 6738

Macbeth leaves Scotland

I've an afternoon flight. I could get a couple of hours in town. But I really can't be arsed. What would I do with my luggage, anyway?

I spend the morning watching crap TV in my hotel room. Then check out at noon exactly. Before that just long enough to be annoying walk. It really is annoying with my full set of luggage.

Strictly speaking, I'm a little too early to check in my bag. But the nice lady at the counter lets me do it, anyway. Great. I don't have to lug all that crap around with me anymore. I shouldn't have brought so many books. But it's almost impossible to guess how many I'll need.

I get myself a sarnie for the plane and an Observer for Dolores in WH Smiths. I say it's for Dolores, but I'll be reading it, too.

Edinburgh airport has the luxury of a Wetherspoons both airside and landside. I choose the latter. I've got a couple of hours to kill. What better place to get out the AK47 and go crazy? Spraying that bastard time with a full clip.

Well blow me. They've got a Mild on:

Strahaven Craigmill Mild, 3.5%, £3.85
This is weird. Getting Mild in an airport. And a Scottish Mild, at that. Dry and slightly malty. A real easy drinker.

Two youths sat behind me keep playing music. A bloke in his 60's takes exception to it. "What are you doing? People are trying to eat and drink here."

It doesn't go down well with the lads. "I'm off to Ibiza. What are you doing?" As if that somehow explains their behaviour. This could turn nasty. I imagine glasses and fists flying. But after a while of arguing across the bar, things calm down. And the lads get back to knocking back pints of cheap Lager.

Time for another pint and some scran.

Stewart Brewing Edinburgh Gold, 4.8%, £3.85
It is a lovely clear gold colour. Mmm that's nice. Soft and with a fair bit of what taste like English hops, also a little underlying sweetness.

I'm tempted to order an all day brunch. But that would be just too much. I can't eat one every day I'm here. I'm tempted by the fish and chips, but eventually plump for beef and ale pie. It's a proper pie, not stew with a pastry lid. If you can't hold it in your hand, it isn't a pie.

I while away the hours reading the paper and slowly sucking down a few pints. Then it's time to go through security. Which thankfully doesn't have much of a queue.

A better flight than on the way out. When all they served was a piece of cake. This time it's an egg sandwich.

Bit of a queue again at Schiphol passport control. But I suppose that does mean I spent less time by the carousel waiting for my bag to appear.

I'm knacked, so I take a taxi home. What an extravagant git I am.

The Turnhouse
Adjacent to Security, First floor food court. Landside
Tel: 0131 344 3030
http://www.edinburghairport.com/shopping-and-eating/restaurants/the-turnhouse

The North

Manchester again

Another Friday, another trip to Schiphol. Not something I look forward to with any great enthusiasm.

The airport is ridiculously overcrowded, though not quite as bad as in May. When it took me two hours to drop off my bag and get through security. But, I now realise that I don't have to queue with the plebs. My silver status in KLM's frequent flyer programme means I can go through the Sky Priority lane, which has far shorter queues. Hooray!

I'm through all the irritating formalities in less than 20 minutes. Which is a miracle.

Having plenty of time – I got here two hours before departure, as advised - I've time for a beer. It might only be 8:30, but different rules apply in airports. My flight departs from pier D. Which just happens to be where the Murphy's Irish pub is located. On the way I eat the egg and bacon sandwich I picked up in the landside Albert Heijn. It cost less than half than what the robbing bastards charge airside.

I settle into a seat at the bar. I've been through here so often that I recognise half the bar staff. How sad is that. Soon a blandish pint of Murphy's Stout is settling itself slowly into my stomach. I have a read of the paper while I sip.

I'm one of the three people who still subscribe to a printed daily newspaper. Mine, NRC Next, is pretty decent. Not rabidly biased like most of the UK press and with articles written by proper, named journalists. It's also good camouflage. Who would suspect that I'm English? With all the Brexit shit, I'm not particularly proud of my nationality. Don't want to be mocked or pitied. Not sure which of those is worse.

Half way down my pint, I get this sudden urge. "Double Jamesons, please." It's going to be a long day. I need some fire in my belly.

I bought that breakfast sarnie for a reason. KLM's food service on their morning flights isn't inspiring: a piece of cake and a little tub of water. I don't eat the cake, as I don't eat refined sugar. Haven't since I was fourteen. Luckily I get a little bottle of red wine to keep up my spirits.

Last time we came to Manchester we flew with Easyjet. Whose flights arrive at Terminal 1. Which is about five miles closer to the airport's railway station.

I'm staying at the Doubletree, handily directly opposite Piccadilly Station. But I don't head directly there. I have a few errands. First, and most important: collecting my train ticket for tomorrow's journey to Sheffield. Then WH Smiths to pick up a copy of Viz, a bottle of water and a bag of crisps. The essentials for a night in Girlchester.

It's only 11:30 and my room isn't ready. "When will it be ready?" I ask. "About one o' clock."

Now there's a dilemma. I've a visit booked to the archives at Manchester Central Library. Should I try to fit it in before or after checking in? I inadvertently make the decision for myself. I've left my cameras in the luggage I've left at the hotel. I can't be arsed to ask them to pull it out again, so I do the only logical thing. I head for the nearest Wetherspoons.

It's on Piccadilly. Not one I've been too before. The young barmaid who serves me is obviously new. Asking colleagues a few times about how to ring stuff up on the till. But she's friendly enough. We all have to start sometime.

It's a bit dark inside which makes reading my Viz tricky. I change seats to somewhere with slightly more light. It helps. A bit.

Thankfully my room is ready when I return. I go up to it to quickly dump my stuff. Inside there's a tray of Partizan beers and some chocolates. I'm a bit puzzled at first. Then remember I'd given the brewery the hotel's address when they offered to send me some beer. And not just any beer. Most of it is their version of 1945 Tetley Mild. I'm looking forward to trying that later.

Luckily the library isn't far and I'm there well before 2 PM. Leaving me more than three hours of frantic snapping. Should be plenty of time. I've only ordered a dozen or so documents.

I've come to love the calm inside archive reading rooms. Something very soothing about them. Though I'm anything but calm, really, as I take photo after photo, limited only by how quickly my camera resets.

"Is this the last?" I ask the nice lady who's ladling out the brewing logs to me. "Yes, that's it" So that's me done. An odd anti-climax. Stupidly, I didn't bring the list of documents I'd requested. I have a nagging feeling that I've missed something. Still, I'm finished more than half an hour before the archives close. And I've only taken 800 photos. I'm such a lightweight.

No time to rest, mind. I've an appointment with John Clarke at the Marble Arch pub at 5:30. It's over the other side of town and by the time I've dumped my posh camera at the hotel – not taking that on a pub crawl with me – I'm running a bit late.

Funnily enough, I've never been to the Marble Arch before. Not sure why. The interior is impressive. And it's pretty crowded. Though I suppose it is Friday night. I eventually manage to spot John. Then I spot something else. On the bar. A pumpclip announcing Imperial Stout. I can't pass that up.

"A pint of Imperial Stout, please."

"Are you sure you want a full pint?" Of course I do. I don't do halves.

John introduces me to Jan, the owner. We chat a while and I suggest she gets her brewer to make a good old fashioned Manchester beer. Like a C Ale. She seems quite keen

After a second pint of Imperial Stout, me and John head over to the Hare and Hounds for a pint of Holts. It's a gorgeous, unspoilt pub with an intact pre-war interior.

I have to admit that the evening is getting a bit hazy. Can't think why. I've only had a couple of pints.

Wetherspoons
49 Piccadilly
+44 161 236 9206
https://www.jdwetherspoon.com/

The Marble Arch
73 Rochdale Rd,
Manchester M4 4HY.
https://marblebeers.com

Tel: +44 161 832 5914

Hare & Hounds
46 Shudehill
Manchester
M4 4AA

Sheffield

I'm not up that early. I said I'd be in Sheffield about one. It's going to be a bit later than that.

I pick up a Cornish nasty and a cheese and onion sandwich in Piccadilly station. I would get a couple of bacon baps from Greggs, but, as I discovered in Edinburgh a couple of weeks ago, they don't do them after eleven. Lunacy. The lust for bacon doesn't end before lunch. It lasts all day. Why do some places serve breakfast all day?

It's lovely ride through the Pennines. And the train doesn't stink. Sheep stud the verdant pastures. Cliffs rear and stone farmhouses skulk sullenly in the dales. Amazingly, the sun is shining. Perfect. One of the things I really miss is the northern countryside. The wild bits. Open moorland scoured by wind and rain. Gets me all emotional just imagining it.

I roll into Sheffield around 12:30. When was I last here? At least 20 years ago, possibly more. How many times have I been here before? Twice, no, three times. Once that weird Newark CAMRA bus trip where I came down from Leeds by train then hitched a ride in the bus back to Newark.

Now I think about it, all the Newark CAMRA trips I went on were crazy. Like the one to Batemans. Where Chris Holmes cancelled at the last minute and my brother had to drive the minibus, even though he was too young. (That tells you how long ago this was.) The tour was brilliant and finished with a great buffet. It was the journey back that was insane. But I'll tell you about that another time. I'm straying too far off topic.

Do you remember me telling you how unaccustomed to hills I am? And how unappreciative, other than as a scenic backdrop to my train journeys. Like many Yorkshire towns, Sheffield is hilly. Very hilly. And the railway station is in a valley. Everywhere is uphill. Including my hotel.

Luckily, my room is ready this time. I dump my shit and jump in a cab. My destination is Hop Hideout, a beer shop where I'm be speaking this evening. That's nice. It's next door to a pub with a Tennant's sign.

My contact is Jules. I ask the man standing behind the counter if he's Jules. "No, I'm not. That's Jules." He says pointing at a young woman. That's confusing. All through our email contact I'd assumed Jules was a man. How wrong I was.

Soon I've a beer in my hand and we're chatting affably away. This is one of the modern type of offie where they also have an on-licence. Pretty sure they would never have stood for this when I were a lad. It's pretty compact, with just a single table and a tiny bar counter.

I can't linger long. We've an appointment at nearby Abbeydale Brewery. Where they're brewing one of my William Younger recipes (1868 No. 1 Ale, in case you're wondering). If we rush we can get there before they're done. Luckily it's not a long walk.

When we arrive the brewer, clad in the traditional wellies and beard, is fiddling around with some spent hops. The brew, it seems, has gone well. It's a pretty long-term project. The beer will be aged in a variety of barrels and be ready for next year's Sheffield Beer Week in March. Which I plan attending. If only to drink that beer.

There's an awful lot of brewery crammed into a rather small space. With more new fermenters recently squeezed in. So they must be doing reasonably well.

Back at the shop, there's time for a few more beers and pie and peas before I give my talk to a small but interested audience. The small and interested perhaps explaining why it takes three hours rather than the usual one. I don't mind. I'm happy to keep talking as long as anyone is listening. Actually, it doesn't even matter if anyone is listening. I love talking about beer.

The attendees – all members of a homebrew club – have brought along beers brewed using recipes in my new Scotland book (available for purchase here). Wettening my dusty words. And dusty throat, too.

When the words have finally dried up, Will, Jules' partner in both senses of the word, drives us back into town and drops me off at my hotel.

The bar is still open. I nip in for a quick nightcap. There's an odd crowd. Mostly fifty-somethings dressed up to the nines. I feel rather scruffy. A bumbling barman makes ordering drinks a longwinded procedure. They don't accept cash, which is OK by me. I can charge it to my room. One less receipt to drive Dolores crazy.

Another busy day shunts me into slumber's soft embrace. I sleep well.

Hop Hideout
448 Abbeydale Rd,
Sheffield S7 1FR.
http://www.hophideout.co.uk/

Abbeydale Brewery
8 Aizlewood Rd,
Sheffield S8 0YX.
Tel: +44 114 281 2712
http://www.abbeydalebrewery.co.uk/

Manchester again, again

A lazy morning staring at Sunday Brunch on the TV. It passes the time.

I have vague plans of eating breakfast in the Wetherspoons on the way to the station. But then I get an email from Jules suggesting we meet at noon in the Sheffield Tap. Bum. No time for brekkie.

Jules has a couple of tickets to Pilcrow's Summer Beer Thing. Will can't make it so she asked me yesterday if I'd fancy going. Squeezing in it should be possible. I had no real plans for my few hours in Manchester, other than going to a pub and eating.

Walking to the station is more fun than walking from it. The best thing about it being in a valley, is whichever direction you come from, it's downhill.

I get myself a sarnie for the train, then try to find Sheffield Tap. After a bit of aimless wandering around, I find a map of the station. Which points me in the right direction and soon I'm standing in the bar staring at a row of handpumps.

"A pint of Jaipur, please." I'm playing it safe. "Do you have pork scratchings?" I ask, hopefully. "Yes. Which flavour would you like?" Flavour? I thought they only came in pig flavour. Evidently they have barbecue and salt and vinegar. When did pork scratchings go all posh?

I realise this is the first pub I've been in since arriving in Sheffield. In almost 24 hours. That's some sort of record.

It's pretty empty, giving me time to admire the lovely surroundings. In an old refreshment room, with all the tilework retained, it's as impressive as any Edwardian pub. After a while Jules turns up and asks: "Do you want to look at the brewery? It's in the next room." I hadn't even realised there was a brewery.

The shiny things are arranged in one half of another equally impressive tiled space. I should have looked more closely at the pumps on the bar. They had several of their own beers on. Oh well, too late for that now. Because we've only time for the one before jumping on the train.

It's a relatively short journey. Made to seem all the shorter by the beers that Jules has brought along with her. I like someone who thinks ahead. Especially beerily thinks ahead.

The event we're headed to is a beer festival outside a pub. The Pilcrow Pub, to be exact. As we walk over there, Jules tells me the pub looks like it's been built by hand. She's not wrong. She could have added "from old pallets" to that description.

It's a single-story wooden building with a pitched roof. Very modern-looking in some ways. But we aren't headed inside. After collecting a glass and some tokens we sit inside the tents pitched outside. That's where all the beer is. Where to start? DIPA, I think. I haven't a great deal of time.

I'm enjoying myself so much, I cut things a bit fine. For catching my plane. Victoria station is close by. I hurry there to pick up a cab. Which takes a worryingly long time to get through town. But I do remember to snap the Royal (formerly Red Tower Lager Brewery) on the way. Not the most scenic of breweries, but one with a place in history nevertheless.

I get to Manchester airport about an hour before my flight is due to leave. But I need to print off my boarding pass and drop off a bag. Which takes a little time.

The queue for security is scarily long. Luckily they come around and ask if anyone has a flight leaving soon. I can move right to the end of the queue.

It's still almost boarding time when I get through all the formalities. Just time to gulp down a quick whisky at the bar and hurry along to my gate. I arrive a minute or two before boarding starts. Perfect timing.

Not having really eaten much today, I wolf down the egg sandwich we're given. Then slowly sip on the red wine.

There's a huge queue at Schiphol passport control. By the time I'm through, my bag is already circling around on the carousel.

I take a taxi home. Feeling knacked I am. And I need to be up at 6:30 for work tomorrow.

Life returns to its iterative norm.

Sheffield Tap
1b, Sheffield Station,
Sheaf St,
Sheffield S1 2BP.
Tel: +44 114 273 7558
http://www.sheffieldtap.com/

The Pilcrow Pub
Sadler's Yard
Hanover Street
Manchester M60 0AB.
http://www.thepilcrowpub.com/

Index

www.ingramcontent.com/pod-product-compliance
Lightning Source LLC
Chambersburg PA
CBHW051722090426
42738CB00010B/2036